MW01200196

# *Love*
# WORTH
## WAITING FOR

## *Rebecca Walker Yount*

For those hoping to find real love
and those who already have

ISBN 978-1-63874-385-9 (paperback)
ISBN 978-1-63874-386-6 (digital)

Christian Faith Publishing
832 Park Avenue
Meadville, PA 16335
www.christianfaithpublishing.com

Cover and engagement photos by Amy Coleman
Wedding photos by Karen Gilmour

Printed in the United States of America

To my beloved husband, Matthew William Yount, and my dear father, Robert Blair Walker, the two men I have loved most in this life.

My husband, Matthew, was and always will be the love of my life. Without a doubt, Matthew made me one of the happiest women to have walked on this earth. In conversation with him one day, I said to Matthew, "You know, I have often watched God answer prayer in remarkable ways for people. But in my opinion, God outdid Himself when He brought the two of us together." I truly meant that.

I remember telling Matthew that someday I hoped to write a book. He responded casually by saying, "Oh yeah! Am I gonna be in it?"

I replied, "Are you kidding? You are the reason *for* it!"

Often I have wondered if I would ever have been blessed to have had Matthew as my husband if it had not been for the faithful prayers of my father. Dad was my cheerleader when life was going especially well and my constant source of encouragement when circumstances became difficult. I was richly blessed to have had a father who regularly and consistently prayed, perhaps more faithfully than any other, for God to send a man such as Matthew into my life.

These two amazing heroes of mine arrived in heaven only six months apart from each other.

# Preface

My husband once told me that he was intrigued by walking through cemeteries and reading the headstones and memorials. He enjoyed calculating how old the people would have been when they passed and reading the inscriptions chosen by someone who likely loved them in this world. Only once did Matthew and I take such a walk together, and I am so grateful that we did. Matthew appreciated the fact that every person who ever breathed air on this earth had a story to tell.

Well, now that my Matthew has been chosen to take up residence in heaven with his Lord, it became *my* honor to choose the words engraved into *his* memorial. Those few words, however, cannot possibly tell his story—or ours. It just so happens that I am biased enough to think that our story is quite spectacular, so I will do my best to tell it.

> You never really know the true value of a
> moment until it becomes a memory.
> —Author unknown

# Acknowledgments

I would like to give special thanks to my Lord and Savior, Jesus Christ, for bringing a truly exceptional man into my life in October of 2010. This book is dedicated to my Matthew's memory…the gentle giant of a man who married me in August of 2011 and went to be with our Lord two years and five months later on January 29 of 2014.

I will always be grateful to my mother, Kathy Walker, without whose intervention, I may never have heard of, or met, the wonderful man who would later become my husband. Along that same line, I will forever be thankful that Mr. Dale Fry and his late wife, Mrs. Nancy Fry, allowed the Lord to use them to arrange for Matthew and me to meet on a blind date in their home.

I also want to thank the family and friends who have expressed to me through the years that my story ought to be told, in hopes that it may be a help and an encouragement to others. Special thanks to one friend in particular who told me many times in the years before I met Matthew, "Becky, I just don't think this is the rest of your story." You were right, Jodie. I had yet to meet Matthew Yount.

I owe a debt of gratitude to my late father, my mother…and also to my sisters, Amy Coleman and Colleen Sexton; their husbands, Aaron and Larry; and my nephews and nieces, Chase, Leanna, Reed, and Allison. I was inexpressibly thankful for the way they excitedly welcomed Matthew into our family. My mom told me that she considered Matthew to be our "icing on the cake." I also remain indebted to them for the way they faithfully kept me in their prayers when I needed them most, following Matthew's death. I can't imagine what I would have done without them during this time when I had no further desire for my life on earth to continue. I still recall with clarity how night after night, for a brief while, either my mom or one of my sisters would take turns spending the night with me when I couldn't bear the thought of being alone again. One other fact I remember just as clearly: each one of them would read the Bible to me the next morning and pray out loud *for* me when I could not find words to speak to God myself. I also remember the times when I was reminded, "Becky, God isn't finished with you. You have a book yet to write."

I want to express heartfelt appreciation to my precious extended "family" of Calvary Baptist Church in Butler, Pennsylvania. I will always be grateful for the way they shared in Matthew's and my joy as we were falling in love and as we married. Just as importantly, I am thankful for the many prayers they prayed to the Lord on my behalf after Matthew was taken to heaven so suddenly. I feel truly blessed to have these wonderful people in my life.

Finally, I would like to thank all of my closest in-laws for their continued love and support. I want to begin by thanking my father-in-law, Carl Yount, and Matthew's only brother, Michael Yount, and his wife, Amy. Michael, Amy, and our nephew and nieces, Aidan, Kathleen, Lindsay, and Claire, frequently sent cards to me throughout every month of the entire first year that we had lost Matthew. They will never realize just how much that thoughtfulness meant to me. I owe special thanks to Matthew's beloved "Grandma Q," the late Dorothy Quesenberry. I am truly honored to have had the privilege of knowing her. And most especially, I want to thank my mother-in-law, Louise Yount. It has been an unexpected blessing for which I will forever be thankful that she and I have developed a special closeness since losing Matthew. This, I am certain, would make my husband extremely proud. My mother-in-law is the closest earthly tie I have to Matthew and has become a treasured friend. She has no idea how it has warmed my heart when she has said to me, "Becky, Matthew would be proud of you."

# Introduction

When, at the age of forty-three, you have never yet married, the dreams you once possessed of finding your "prince charming" and living *happily ever after* have a way of fading off into a ridiculous waste of time and energy. Instead, you begin trying to wrap your head around the idea that you might likely end up the stereotypical old maid.

Now don't get me wrong. I know as well as anyone does that not every person who walks the face of the earth is destined to marry. I also know that some who *do* marry wish they never had…yet the dream of having a husband of my own remained.

My name is Becky Yount and this is my story.

# Chapter 1

This was the day I had dreamed about all of my life! I was standing in the sunlit foyer of the church, dressed in a beautiful white, chiffon-and-satin gown. My right hand was resting on the arm of my father, clad in a black tuxedo, and my left hand carried a fragrant bouquet of white roses and lilies. Side by side, my father and I stood waiting behind a pair of heavy wooden doors. We could hear the wedding music playing; and in just another moment, those doors would be opened. I would then begin the long-awaited walk down the aisle to join the tall, dark, and handsome man waiting for me at the front of the church auditorium. Today, this man would become my husband.

Yes, I am well aware that this same scene has taken place countless times in countless places, the world over. But this wedding was different. This was *my* wedding, the wedding that I had nearly ceased to hope would ever take place. I had celebrated my forty-fourth birthday only six days before. I had not ever been married, nor had I ever lived with a "significant other."

One other particular fact was even more amazing to me. My handsome groom also had never married or lived with someone that he had been dating. Neither he nor I had ever had a physical relationship which could have resulted in having children—not with anyone else nor with each other. I myself have never heard of another couple of similar ages whose situation was the same—certainly not in the twenty-first century.

But if you'd like to be further befuddled, here is a little-known fact that I must add to the story so that you can understand the slim likelihood that I would yet marry. By the age of forty-four, I still had never been kissed. (Yes, you read that correctly.) I hadn't even held hands with a man, not even a *young* man, when I was dating as a teen. I also made sure to never date alone or to even ride in a vehicle alone with a man. If the dates did not take place at a group activity, I would arrange to have another couple along. All of these rules and boundaries were in place because I had established a goal when I began dating at the age of seventeen. I wanted to be fully and completely pure for the husband that I hoped to marry one day. I wanted to enjoy every romantic touch of any kind with one man and one man only. And after stating that, I'm sure you understand that men were not lining up at the door to date me.

The fact that Matthew and I had both stayed single for so long was surely not due to lack of dating opportunities, for we both had plenty of those through the years. Each of us also had family and friends who thought enough of us that they would endeavor to set us up on dates with *prospective candidates* as often as the opportunities might arise. And in both cases, we tried to be open to the possibilities. Yet I will be honest with you. We admitted to each other that we were both terribly "picky" and we knew it. Speaking for myself, I had finally decided that I wanted to stop looking for a man that I could live *with*. I wanted to find the man that I couldn't live *without*.

# Chapter 2

As a ten-year-old girl, I had come to the realization that I was a sinner in need of forgiveness after being taught that the Lord Jesus Christ had loved me enough to die on a cross, paying the penalty for my sin. At this time, I had knelt down beside my bed and asked Christ to forgive my sins and to be my personal Savior. A few short years after that, I became part of a good solid youth group in a great little Bible-believing church. I sincerely desired to live the kind of life that would make my Savior proud. In my youth group, I was taught that it was important to ask for God's help in choosing a man to become my husband one day. It was also strongly recommended that I only date the kind of young man that I would want to marry.

Well, I earnestly tried to keep this in mind as I became old enough to date. I had even decided that I would have no physical contact with young men—saving myself, in every sense of the word, for that one man who would become my husband.

To be completely honest, these "rules" were not terribly difficult for me to keep, for many reasons. First of all, I was very quiet and reserved. I didn't even have my first date until I was a high school senior at the age of seventeen. My first boyfriend was from an excellent Christian family. Because he was away at a Bible college in the state of Indiana, most of our dating was done through letters. When we were together in person, he treated me in a respectful and gentlemanly fashion. For the several months that we dated, he was the perfect first boyfriend.

Then it became *my* turn to go to college. I wanted to become a schoolteacher.

Upon enrolling in a Bible college in Massillon, Ohio, I had decided that I hated having the reputation of always being quiet and shy. Because I would be living in a college dormitory in another state, I realized that these people didn't know me yet, and this would be the perfect time for me to *come out of my shell.* Those years were fun and exciting, and I considered them to be some of my happiest. I didn't have a "serious" boyfriend until the beginning of my second year in college when I met the most handsome young man I believe I had ever seen up to that point.

This man, only two years older than me, arrived on campus during my sophomore year of college. I came into contact with him initially because he stopped to ask for my help. He was dropping off his fiancée at the door of the ladies' dorm and was helping to unload her things from the car. He explained that they were both enrolling in college but that she was already homesick and threatening not to stay. Then he asked me to try to befriend her. I do not remember seeing her after that day. I did hear that she quickly went home.

This very good-looking man, however, stayed.

What I did shortly after was terribly unwise. I began to pray that God would cause this man (we'll call him Brandon) and his fiancée to break off their engagement. I would pray almost daily concerning this matter and would tell the Lord, that because I knew He was not an unkind God, surely He would arrange for me to get to date Brandon. Then I would say that if He didn't plan to make this happen, it would have been downright cruel for God to let this man and I meet in the first place. (I, more or less, insisted that God do what I asked, and I did this almost every day for several months.)

Much to my amazement, Brandon, who had become increasingly friendly with me throughout that fall semester, drove to Pennsylvania on our Christmas break, showing up at one of the services at my church. His goal was to surprise me and to let me know that he was no longer engaged and would love for us to start dating.

I returned to college after Christmas break to find my first name shoveled through the snow in mammoth-sized letters across the front lawn of the men's dorm. The girls on campus couldn't wait to ask if I was the Becky whose name was shoveled in the snow. After asking who had done the shoveling, I knew it was meant for me, and I was elated!

Brandon and I instantly became a couple. Regularly, he would leave me handwritten romantic notes, scented with his cologne. Often he would have flowers or gifts delivered to me. This man was an incredible "romantic." I knew I was the envy of many girls, and that felt strange yet wonderful.

We became engaged that summer and planned a wedding for the summer following my college graduation. Life was very exciting! Several of our friends would also be marrying that same summer and some had planned, as we had, to remain in that college town. I felt like life couldn't get much better…until the week we were to marry.

After graduating with my bachelor's degree in education, I moved back home to Pennsylvania to prepare for the wedding, and Brandon moved into the apartment in Massillon, Ohio, that he and I would share after we married.

As time drew near to our wedding date, I began to notice that some of our conversations were becoming awkward and uncomfortable. It almost seemed as though Brandon was hiding something from me. At that point in my life, however, I mistakenly believed everyone to be inherently honest. I didn't even consider that Brandon may have things he didn't want me to know. I was a very naive twenty-one-year-old.

During a phone conversation with my fiancé three days before our wedding date, Brandon had told me just enough truth to let me see that I had been greatly deceived about the reality of his financial situation. After speaking to my mother about this phone call, she quickly recommended that I call my pastor's wife to talk with her about the hurt and confusion that Brandon's conversation had created. I made that call to my pastor's wife, explaining the situation to her, and she responded with, "Honey, you and Brandon need to meet with your preacher."

Brandon knew that he had upset me and called back to apologize for not being honest and upfront with me. I asked if he would make the two-and-a-half-hour trip to Pennsylvania just as quickly as he could so that we could meet with my pastor (who had been conducting premarital counseling for us). Brandon explained that he just couldn't miss another day of work since he would already be taking time off for the wedding. He would come on Thursday, the day of our rehearsal, as planned. We could meet with my pastor early in the day.

Brandon and I had together planned for a honeymoon in Tennessee. I would later be informed (by someone other than my fiancé) that Brandon had no intention of taking me to Tennessee but instead to a campground nearby. And although the following fact makes no difference one way or the other, Brandon knew that I hated camping. At this campsite, however, he was going to set up a tent for us to spend our wedding night in. I was later told that he had already borrowed the tent from his sister and had it stashed away in the trunk of his car. I suppose he was planning to *surprise* me with this change of plans after we became husband and wife.

During the course of the meeting in my pastor's office that Thursday, many questions were directed to Brandon, and he chose that day to come clean. Brandon had not lied about finances *only*. Some of his lies were little and some were large, but lying had become a habitual way of life for him...and he was so good at it that I had been completely unaware. Near the end of the lengthy meeting, my pastor waved a hand toward me and asked Brandon in an exasperated tone, "Do you even love her?"

I can still picture Brandon hanging his head, as he answered, "No...not like I should to marry her."

My heart lay broken in pieces on the floor of the pastor's office at the church in which we had planned to marry the next day. We canceled the wedding.

Brandon chose to drop out of college even though he had one more year to finish. He moved close to my parents' home and rented a place to stay in while he proved to me that he could change his ways. We continued to date for the next many months...just long enough for me to see through a facade that I wasn't able to recognize before. In the end, I had simply lost all respect that I once had for him, and I realized that I would never again be able to trust him.

Although I was terribly hurt by Brandon, I truly have never hated him. He was a man with many wonderful qualities, who would have been a great husband and a great father, if only he could have conquered some serious issues with dishonesty. Along that line, my parents both saw him quite a few years ago, at a church they were visiting, a couple hours away from where I live. Brandon introduced my parents to his wife, who I was told looked a lot like me, and pointed out his little girls. He pulled my dad aside and stated, "Mr. Walker, I am not the man I used to be." I was truly grateful to hear that, and I am truly *hopeful* that he has become a man of character.

# Chapter 3

I remember my mother telling me that she didn't see me smile for two solid months after Brandon and I broke up. I had been devastated! I hate to admit the hundreds of times through the years to come that I doubted I had done the right thing. Most times I believed that I had missed my chance—that Brandon had been the one meant for me, and that I had made too big a deal of dishonesty. I often wondered where that left me when it came down to *God's will* in regard to a husband for me. I have always strongly believed that God has one particular person that He has hand-picked for each of us to marry, if marrying is His will for us at all. Because I knew Brandon had married someone else, I wondered if that meant that I would have to settle for second-best. I was very mistaken in this thinking, as I would find out twenty-three years later.

If my wedding had taken place as planned that summer of 1988, I would have moved to Ohio. Now that my engagement was permanently broken off, however, I had to quickly find employment back at home. I was hired part-time as a teacher's assistant in the private Christian school I had graduated from. For a year and a half, I would help out in the third- and fourth-grade classroom at Calvary Academy every morning. Then I would go to work in the afternoons as a delivery driver for a local deli in downtown Butler.

After that year and a half came to a close, I chose to go back to college—first of all, because there was no one for me to date at home. Secondly, I had been informed that there was no possibility of a continued teaching position at Calvary Academy for me. I don't recall there being any other Christian schools in the area at that time, and I really had no desire to teach in a public school.

Since breaking off my engagement with Brandon, my life seemed to be floundering. It felt as if things were going from bad to worse. I saw no hope here to find a future husband and no hope here as a teacher. I needed something to change. I needed something to improve. And at that time, my sister Amy was planning to enroll in Pensacola Christian College in Pensacola, Florida. This college was very large, unlike Massillon Baptist College in Ohio where I had earned my bachelor's degree. I decided to enroll along with my sister. PCC was well-known for its excellent teacher's training program, and I knew I could benefit from that.

I didn't have the money to put toward earning a master's degree. At this point, I just wanted to gather all the knowledge I could in a year's time, hoping that the additional training might help me to land a teaching position in a Christian school somewhere...anywhere. I took out a personal loan to get me through the first semester. Then I took out a student loan for the second.

Just before that school year ended, I received a call from the school administrator of Calvary Academy, where I had been a teacher's assistant back home in Pennsylvania. He informed me that their third- and fourth-grade teacher had turned in her resignation and was moving away from the area with her husband. They needed to replace her before the start of the next school year. He asked how I was doing in my student-teaching courses. Since I had been assigned to work in a fourth-grade classroom, I asked that master teacher to give me a written critique following my student-teaching in her classroom. After the school administrator back home had heard the grades I had earned and read the critiques the master teacher had written, I was quickly offered the position back in Pennsylvania. I never would have expected to be returning there.

That fall of 1991, I began pouring my heart and my life into teaching. I had known from the time I was seventeen that I was meant to be a teacher. I was now twenty-three and my career had finally begun. I *loved* what I was doing!

During my year of college in Pensacola, I had dated quite a bit. As a young schoolteacher and on into the next decade of my life, I continued to date as opportunities presented themselves. I also was blessed to have many friends and acquaintances who would try to fix me up with single Christian men whom they knew. I would compare every man, however, to the very handsome, charming, and romantic fiancé that Brandon had been to me; and no one quite matched up.

Then I agreed to let a former college professor give my phone number to a man that I'll call Luke.

Luke lived in North Dakota and was a youth pastor in his church. He had never married; and if memory serves me correctly, I believe he was almost forty. I was in my early to mid-thirties by that time. We couldn't easily meet in person, so we talked on the phone often. He was a sincere Christian, and I loved that. We really hit it off on the phone. He and I talked often for about a month and a half. He had a great sense of humor; and the more we got to know about each other, the more we felt that perhaps we needed to meet in person.

That was when Luke informed me that he had chosen to follow the rules of "courtship." (I've heard others refer to this as "betrothal.") He explained that he believed dating to be *wrong* because he felt that "breaking up" only sets people up for divorce when a disagreement comes along after they're married. I realize that many good Christians believe this to be true. I, however, completely disagree and had to tell him so. I wholeheartedly believe that every man I've ever dated has helped to mold my life in some way or other, helping me to become the person that I now am. And keeping physical contact out of a dating relationship, such as I had done all along, protected me from any regrets or scars of that nature. So to me, dating was not only harmless but also normal, healthy, and good.

Luke did not agree. He had his pastor call and talk to me. Then he sent me a recorded sermon that he himself had preached to the teens in his youth group in support of courtship. Because Luke was an adult man when he came to believe that he should no longer *date*, Luke had asked his pastor to take on the role of a father in a situation of this sort. If Luke felt that I would make a good wife for him, I had to gain the approval of his pastor. Then we would become engaged to marry. *After* that, we would endeavor to get to know each other before the wedding date. Love would *eventually* come into the arrangement—if not *before* marriage, then surely after. If Luke's pastor (in ordinary cases, this would be the father in the home) did not agree that I would be the right kind of wife for him, Luke would continue on his search. Or perhaps the pastor would recommend a young woman to Luke for his consideration.

During the course of the phone call placed by Luke's pastor to me, it appeared that I was considered an appropriate candidate to be Luke's wife. This whole idea, however, did not sit well with me. I finally explained to Luke that I had never been good at pretending. I had every intention of becoming a supportive wife. And because he was a youth pastor, I was quite certain that somewhere along the line, a young teenage girl in his ministry would come to me, not understanding why she was not allowed to date. In a case such as that, I could not pretend that I agreed with the stipulations of courtship; and therefore, I could not be a support to him in his ministry. Luke was a *good* man who completely deserved to be happily married to a woman who would not disagree with him on a matter that was so close to his heart.

After trying to make this as clear as possible, I asked that we end the relationship since I was assured that my mind was not about to be changed on the matter. We ended the phone call kindly and civilly. We voiced appreciation for all the time spent trying to get to know each other and genuinely wished each other well. Then it was over.

Or so I thought.

Several weeks later, a tall nicely dressed gentleman by the name of Luke showed up at the school where I taught, asking to see me. Until that day, we had never met. He had driven alone from North Dakota to Pennsylvania to convince me that I needed to reconsider a future relationship with him. He stayed in the area for eight days, coming to have lunch with me at the school during those days and arranging special dinners with me every evening. Luke was also a music director at his church and had written me a song, which he would sing to piano music as he presented me with a bouquet of flowers. This would be the final attempt to convince me before heading home to North Dakota.

Everything he did was incredibly flattering and sweet. But it did not change the fact that Luke believed strongly in the idea that dating was wrong and that marriages needed to be *arranged*. I might have been able to compromise on this, if it weren't for two nagging factors. As stated before, if I were to become this youth pastor's wife, I would completely disapprove of Luke's teaching of courtship to his teens. And secondly, if we were to become parents, I knew myself enough to know that I would not be in favor of my children having their father help to *choose* their future spouse. I wanted to raise my children to love the Lord, their Creator, enough that they would be able to seek God alone for His guidance in choosing the mate that He had planned for them. Then we, as parents, would certainly be able to give our *approval* of *their* choice. I wanted the same for my future children as I wanted for myself. I wanted to marry because I was head over heels in love, not because a partnership with a particular man *made good sense*.

And so, once again, I had to explain my feelings to this well-intentioned man…but this time, in person. It was difficult for me to say; and it had to be hurtful for him to hear, especially after spending so much time, money, and energy on the trip to Pennsylvania. It was almost surely out of hurt that he said the following words to me, which haunted me for several years to come. He looked intently into my eyes and slowly and sternly said, "Becky, be really sure that you want to turn down this opportunity. You *have* to realize that neither one of us is getting any younger. This could be your last chance to marry, you know."

Years later, when I was at a church service in another state while on vacation, I saw Luke's name listed in a bulletin, along with the name of the wife he had married. They were serving as missionaries in Africa.

I was still living on my own.

# Chapter 4

**M**ore time went by. I was tired of being alone. I was tired of being *lonely*. I felt I had waited patiently long enough, hoping that God would bring me the kind of husband I had prayed for since the time I was twenty-one.

I was then informed that my brother-in-law had invited a visitor to come with him to one of our evening church services. My brother-in-law knew this man from work. I was told that he was one of the kindest and most charming men I could ever hope to meet but that he had messed his life up in almost any way one could do so. I gathered from that description that I ought to have no interest in him.

On the evening that he chose to visit our church, I specifically remember my family being seated in the same pew that the visitor was in. We were all introduced, and I remember thinking that this man was better-looking than I expected he would be. For sake of a name, we'll call him Chad.

Chad soon began coming to church services on a regular basis. Because my brother-in-law was endeavoring to help Chad turn his life around, there were times that I would go to visit my sister and brother-in-law at their home and he would show up there also. Of course, this meant that we talked. Chad asked my age and found out that I was six years older than he. I had been told initially that he was very charming, and that was certainly true. Instead of being turned off by the fact that I was older, he seemed to consider that a bit of a challenge to him. I did make an effort to keep my distance because it was easy to tell that he was quite a player.

My concerns seemed to be over when Chad admitted himself into a recovery program for substance abuse. This took him to the Midwest for a period of many months.

When he returned home, however, Chad was clean-cut and sharply dressed, appearing to be a whole new man. He seemed to have a genuine desire to serve the Lord and to make his life count for something worthwhile. He wanted to get involved in some sort of ministry at our church and was allowed, with the oversight of a former pastor, to begin a program for people who battled addictions in our area. These meetings would be housed in our church building every Friday night. He was also placed in charge of the Sunday school bus route that I had worked on every Saturday and Sunday for many years. His involvement in this second ministry would make it impossible for me to keep distance from him. We would be required to work together in the same ministry for hours at a time, every weekend, bringing children to Sunday school and church.

What I intended to not allow soon began to take place. I was beginning to fall for someone who carried more baggage and more scars than anyone I had ever personally known. And to beat all, I realized that I wasn't really sure I cared to stop where my heart was trying to go. What I did know was that I was tired of doing what I believed was right, all the while hoping that God would bring a wonderful man into my life. I was now in my late thirties. I had prayed countless prayers for countless years, and God had not come through for me.

Sometimes Chad would call me, and we would talk for a short while on the phone, but mostly he would send text messages. I would welcome these calls and texts even though I always refused to go out with him on dates. In spite of my continued rejections, it was through these forms of private communication that he told me frankly that he loved me and had been working to become the kind of man who would deserve to marry a lady like myself. I did not admit that I was falling in love with him, yet I knew that I was doing just that.

It was such an odd kind of relationship. The feelings that he claimed to have for me were never spoken or made obvious around other people. This should have been a red flag to me, but at this point in my life, I was enjoying the secret soft-spoken advances of this handsome man. We had a close-knit church which has always felt like a large family, yet no one would ever have guessed that Chad told me often how badly he was hoping that I would one day return his love.

Everyone in the church *was*, however, aware that a certain *other* woman was boldly and unashamedly working to win *his* attention. This woman, who was a struggling addict (I'll refer to her as Carla), had been invited by Chad to attend the Friday night recovery program that he had begun at our church. In short time, she was coming to church services on Sunday mornings, Sunday evenings, and Wednesday nights as well. I would like to tell you that she had honorable reasons for attending these services so faithfully. Her provocative dress and manner spoke otherwise, however. She was a divorcee, clearly in search of finding another husband, and had firmly set her sights on Chad.

Many times I tried to counsel Chad on this matter. He would confide in me, and I would warn him that she was not the kind of woman who would help him in his intentions to stay clean and to become a stronger man, morally. I would tell him that he needed to push her away, and he would claim that he had tried and it hadn't worked. Through all of this, he continued to assure me that he didn't want her. He wanted me.

Chad invited me to go to our church's adult Christmas dinner as his date, and this particular year, I finally said, "Yes." It then became easier to let my guard down and attend some other events with him that summer. We went to see fireworks in Pittsburgh and spent a day at a county fair. By this time, he was calling my parents "Mom" and "Dad." I had decided that it was time for me to invite my sister and brother-in-law over for dinner because I had something I needed to tell them.

After dinner, I informed my sister and brother-in-law that I had decided to tell Chad that I had fallen in love with him. Up to that point, I had never admitted this to be true. Because I had always been open with Amy and considered her to be my closest confidante, I wanted her approval. Because I respected Aaron's opinion, I desired his approval as well. They both listened to me, with straight faces, having little to say. We all knew what we expected to happen as soon as I shared my feelings with Chad. There was likely to be a wedding…and soon.

You know, as I think back on this time in my life, I fully knew that Chad was not the type of man I had saved myself for. It was strikingly obvious that he did not have the character or the moral fiber of a man that I should marry. There were so many things wrong with this picture, and I knew it. But I clearly remember thinking that I was tired of waiting for God to bring me a husband. In my opinion, it was time to take matters into my own hands because I *could*. Here before me was a handsome and charming man who voiced his love for me, when he had no certainty that I would ever return that love. And all the while, he had another woman openly throwing herself at him. It was flattering to think that he wanted *me*.

If truth be told, I knew that a marriage between Chad and me would almost certainly not last very long. Yet even that didn't really matter. I knew that God had heard the many prayers I had prayed through the years. He had chosen to let those prayers go unanswered. And I had *had it*! By this time, I had turned forty, and I wanted to be loved by a man, if only for a little while.

Very soon after informing Amy and Aaron of my plans to confess my love to Chad, my brother-in-law caught up with me as I walked toward my parked car after an evening church service. We stood along the edge of the parking lot, under the shade of a large maple tree, and he had a talk with me that I have never forgotten. Aaron commenced to say, "Becky, your sister and I love you. I *promise you* that I know far more about Chad than you possibly can. And because of that, I want you to realize that this will be the biggest mistake you will ever make in your life. So when your world comes crashing down around your feet one day, as it surely will, your sister and I will still be here for you *because* we love you."

I had no words to say, but I had much to think about.

After arriving home (I believe it might have been that very evening), my phone rang. It was not Chad. It was Carla. She said very sharply and abruptly, "Do you know that Chad loves you?"

I answered softly, "Yes, I do."

She followed with "Do you know that he's *in love* with you?"

I replied, "Yes."

She went on to say, "Well, I'm tired of hearing about it! *I* love *him* and he tells me all the time that he doesn't want to be with me because he wants to be with you. So I think it's time you know what he's been doing behind your back!" This angry woman proceeded to tell me personal, private things that she and Chad had done which made my face redden and my ears burn. Carla was proud to say that she would often drive herself to his house because she knew he was discouraged. Her main desire was to make him forget his worries by doing all the things that only a woman could—and all the things that she knew I never *would* while I was yet unmarried. She boasted that she had gone to him with these intentions time and time again.

The situation that I now found myself in was not God's fault. The blame was all mine and I knew it. I had chosen to give my heart to a man that I should never have been interested in. Nonetheless, my heart was deeply damaged.

After this, I did have one more opportunity to speak privately and in person with Chad. Carla had been quick to inform him about her phone call to me. For this reason, when we were given the chance to meet, Chad looked at me with pain in his eyes and said, "I'm so sorry." He dropped his gaze to the floor.

I responded, "I had just informed my family that I was going to tell you I had fallen in love with you in spite of all my efforts *not* to."

He became visibly emotional and replied, "I didn't know."

He then hung his head again and we both cried.

Chad moved out of my life shortly after that.

My heart felt like it had been ripped into shreds. In hindsight, however, I happen to believe that God, in His omniscient wisdom, had to allow that situation to blow wide open in such a horrible fashion. For a fact, this was for my own best interest. You see, at that time of my life, I had lost all desire to hold out, in hopes that God's answer to my prayers was yet to come. I was convinced that either God had never intended for me to marry (and I didn't like that thought) or I had already missed the "right one" when I turned away one of the other two men who would have married me. Maybe I had just been too picky.

My God up in heaven knew, however, that I would not meet *His* choice for my life until three years later.

# Chapter 5

I only remember meeting a few single people throughout my entire life who have seemed to be perfectly content in never marrying. This attitude had never fit *me*, however. Always, in the back of my mind, I would cling to something that my aunt Penny had once told me. She had said to me years before, "Becky, I believe that if God does not intend for a particular person to marry, He will take that desire away from them. So if you continue to *want* to be married, I would not give up hope that He still has someone out there waiting to meet you."

The next two-and-a-half years or so were very low times for me. I had given up all hope in having a husband. I had lost all joy in life. I had even begun to pray that the Lord would let me die. When God quickly reminded me that I had four young nephews and nieces to watch as they grew up, I would tell Him that I could observe them from heaven. I just didn't want to live on this earth any longer.

My former pastor, who had recently resigned yet remained a faithful member of our church, noticed that I was struggling. He stopped me one Sunday, while walking down the hallway of our church building, to ask how I was doing. After listening to my answer, he told me something that I needed to hear. He said, "Becky, because you had once *chosen* to give your heart to Chad, you may very well have to make a conscious *choice* to take it back." He reminded me that if God still had a husband for me somewhere in my future, then that husband would deserve *all* of my heart, not what was left over.

So I did that. I chose to take my heart back, and I asked the Lord to repair the damage and to make my heart whole again.

While I was at it, I asked Him to once again help me find joy in this life.

Well, God didn't only help me find joy. He brought into my life happiness such as I had never known before.

# Chapter 6

I was in my classroom one school day in early October of 2010 when my cell phone rang. My third- and fourth-grade students were on recess so I was able to answer the call. It was my mother. She said she had something to tell me but warned that I might get upset with her. I replied, "Well, go ahead. Talk to me." She told me that a blind date had been arranged, if I would agree to it. I don't remember what my response to her statement was, but I do know that instead of being upset, I found that I was *excited*. Honestly, I hadn't really expected I would date again. I was now forty-three years old. This opportunity was an unexpected surprise.

Of course, I wanted to know how the situation came about, so my mother began to explain. She and my dad had gone to visit some longtime friends of ours that they had fallen out of touch with for several years. For a long period of time *before*, however, this family and my family had been quite close while we had been members of the same church. My sisters and I had even gone to (and graduated from) our Christian school along with their sons.

My mom and dad had heard that the lady of the home, Nancy Fry, had been fighting brain cancer and that her husband, Dale, was doing his best to keep her in their home for as long as he possibly could. My parents went to visit, hoping to be an encouragement to both of them. But as it would later become incredibly obvious, God chose that day and that visit to begin the makings of my own personal long-awaited love story. And I cannot wait to tell it!

Here we go!

My parents were warmly welcomed into Mr. and Mrs. Fry's home and invited to sit down for a visit. After the four had been conversing for a while, my mom decided to ask something she was curious to know. Because Mr. and Mrs. Fry would often sing duets together when they attended *our* church, my mom casually asked if they still sang together in the Baptist church they were now attending. Mr. Fry answered, "No, Nancy doesn't always remember the words. But *I* still sing in choir, next to a man named Matthew." Well, to that, Mrs. Fry perked up. She turned to my mother and said, "Oh, Kathy, every time I see Matthew, I wish he could meet your Becky!"

Here I have to pause long enough to explain how amazing it is to me that this comment came from her lips. It was known that Mrs. Fry's short-term memory had become rather altered by this time because of the cancer in her brain. To think of her mentioning that she wished Matthew and I could meet still gives me chills when I think of it yet today.

My mom then turned to Mr. Fry and said, "Dale, tell me more about this Matthew." He explained that he didn't know Matthew well, but he liked what he knew of him. Mr. Fry said that Matthew had never been married. He had moved to the area just three years before for work, and he had a good job. Matthew had immediately begun attending the church that the Frys were members of and was faithful to the services there. He knew Matthew was a bit younger than I but didn't think there was too much of an age difference.

My mom was intrigued and asked if Mr. Fry would question Matthew to see if he would be willing to meet me. Mr. Fry quickly responded, "No. I've never been a matchmaker. I don't like when people get into *my* business, and I would rather not get into someone else's."

But my mom has never been one to give up easily. She quickly asked him, "Don't you love my daughter?"

Mr. Fry's response was: "That's not fair. You know I do." My mom went on to ask if he would then make a one-time exception and talk to Matthew. No promises were made, but he did say he would consider.

That very Wednesday night, Mr. Fry did what my mother had asked. He told Matthew that he had a friend he would like him to meet. He went on to say that I had never been married and that I was a third- and fourth-grade teacher at a private Christian school in the area. He also explained that there was a bit of an age difference between us. Matthew later told me that he had only asked Mr. Fry two questions. He first asked, "Is she younger than eighteen?"

Mr. Fry smiled as he replied, "No."

Then Matthew asked, "Is she older than fifty?"

When Mr. Fry answered no to the second question as well, Matthew said, "All right then." Matthew told Mr. Fry to let me know that Mondays and Fridays would work best for him.

Mr. Fry and I then talked on the phone the following Wednesday for the first time. I gave him a few dates that would work for me. Because of Mrs. Fry's health, he was hoping that Matthew and I would be willing to meet at their home for dessert one evening.

The following Sunday, I got another call from Mr. Fry. He informed me that after discussing with Matthew the dates that I had listed as possibilities, Matthew had chosen the first available one, which was the very next day, October 11.

## Chapter 7

I don't know if you have ever been on a blind date or not, but I had been on plenty. And I must tell you, they're not all pretty! In fact, the older I became, the more depressing a blind date could be. If a man anywhere near my own age had not yet married, within moments after meeting, it was normally very obvious as to *why* he hadn't. Sometimes a man's looks told it all because you could easily see that he had long ago stopped putting any effort into his appearance. And sometimes the man was just awfully *odd*, if you know what I mean. (Yes, I do realize that when tables are turned, *men* probably feel the same about meeting a *woman* who hasn't married by her mid-thirties to early forties.)

Well, nothing was said to me about Matthew's looks, which led to a certain assumption, if you understand my meaning. On Sunday night, October 10, I told a handful of my closest friends and work associates that I was going on a blind date the following evening. Of course, they wanted to hear what I knew about this man. Some asked if I had heard what he looked like. Many eyebrows were raised when I responded, "I've heard nothing about his looks." *They* were thinking what *I* was thinking! I responded to their misgivings by saying, "You know, I've already decided that I'll be pleasantly surprised if he doesn't weigh four hundred pounds and if he's not bald. And if he *is* one or both of those things, I'll have a good story to tell you tomorrow!" The way I looked at it, I knew I could have a nice time being with Mr. and Mrs. Fry who I hadn't seen in a very long while.

I figured that if this date went as so many other blind dates had gone before, I would simply make the best of it.

As a sidenote, I told my students at school on Monday that I would let them in on a secret. I told them that I was going on a blind date that evening. I asked if they knew what I meant by a "blind date." One of my third-graders piped up and said, "I know! It means you've got a date with a blind dude!" Although she was a little confused on the matter, it made me smile.

Monday evening arrived.

I had always been known for either arriving at a destination or event *exactly* at the time a function was to begin…or a bit late. I was never *early* to anything. That night I was so pleased with myself! I had arrived at 6:30 p.m., right on time.

I rang the doorbell, and Mr. Fry welcomed me into their home. I found out that this blind date of mine was already seated in the living room, waiting. I would soon find out that Matthew was never late for *anything*. He would rather be thirty minutes early for an appointment than to be a minute late.

I walked with my host down a narrow hallway which led into their living room. Then I saw him. Matthew was walking slowly out of the living room and into the hallway, coming toward me to shake my hand. He was not at *all* what I expected!

This very tall handsome man was clean-cut, freshly shaven, and broad-shouldered, with a full head of dark-brown hair. He surely wasn't bald and he surely wasn't heavy! He was nicely dressed in a long-sleeved blue dress shirt and black dress pants. Matthew was well-mannered and intelligent, as I would soon discover. I remember thinking that he had a great smile and beautiful dark-brown eyes. Only moments before, I hadn't had a glimmer of hope whatsoever that I might find this man to be attractive. Well, I had been wrong!

During the course of the evening, I learned that Matthew had majored in history while earning his bachelor's degree at Edinboro University. He then had gone on to earn a master's degree in library and information sciences at the University of Pittsburgh. He had taken a job as supervisor for the Archives of the United States Steel

Corporation. This man had even acquired a career in the field of study he had trained for! I was completely interested.

At one point, the four of us were seated around the kitchen table. I was positioned directly opposite Matthew; and the longer we talked, the more I was quite sure that he was much younger than I. I couldn't stand the suspense any longer. I said, "Matthew, I've got to ask you a question. I have no idea how old you are. Would you mind telling me?"

He replied matter-of-factly, "Sure! I'm thirty-four."

I sighed softly and asked, "Do you know how old I am?"

He replied, "No."

I turned to the seventy-year-old gentleman seated to my left and said, "Mr. Fry, I made sure you knew my age and asked you to please tell Matthew."

Mr. Fry simply leaned back in his chair, folded his arms across his chest, shrugged his shoulders, and smugly grinned from ear to ear.

I turned back to face Matthew and said, "Well, I think you should know, but I don't want to tell you because you'll want to stand up and walk right out of here."

I distinctly remember Matthew leaning forward across the table a bit toward me as he said, "Then you don't need to tell me."

Well, I did tell him. I said, "I'm forty-three." I was so glad that I was looking directly into Matthew's eyes as I spoke because I could tell that he was clearly surprised. (Later, I would read about this conversation in one of his journals. In *his* words, he was "stunned.")

His response to *me* was "You don't *look* forty-three!"

While his reaction made me feel flattered, I now felt it was pointless to hope that Matthew and I might date again after tonight. I was nine years older than he.

Due to the fact that it was a weeknight, I didn't want to stay too late. I thought it would be good to leave around ten o'clock in the evening. I was teaching the next day, and I found out that Matthew had to drive over an hour to get home. He also had to go to work the following day. I excused myself about three-and-a-half hours after our date had begun so that I could head home. I asked Matthew if he was also ready to leave or if I should say my goodbye in the living room where we had just finished visiting. Matthew said that he was planning to stay and talk with the Frys a bit longer. I rose from the couch where we were both seated and reached out to shake Matthew's hand. He stood as well. I thanked him for agreeing to meet me. I told him that I had really enjoyed having the chance to get to know him a little. Then I said, "Goodbye."

Matthew grasped my hand in return but said, "Let's not say goodbye. How 'bout, 'See you later'?"

In response to that comment, Mrs. Fry enthusiastically interjected, "That's right!"

Mr. Fry smiled and said that he would walk me to the door.

As this kind older gentleman opened my car door for me, he could hardly wait to ask, "Well, what did you *think*?"

I told him that I had had a wonderful time and that Matthew was definitely the kind of man I would love to get to know, but I was afraid that the age difference was too great. I was leaving everything in Matthew's ballpark from here. Mr. Fry asked if he had permission to pass my phone number on to Matthew.

I replied, "Of course!"

After returning inside, Mr. Fry told Matthew that he had permission to give him my phone number. To that, Matthew responded, "I'm just unsure about the difference in our ages. I would rather do some praying about it first. I just need some time."

That was Monday night. Matthew told me later that he had prayed about the situation for two days and had also talked to some close family members concerning our age difference. Matthew later explained that he had really wanted his grandma's opinion. She had responded, "Well, Matthew, you have some very strong beliefs about God and the Bible. Do you think this girl shares those beliefs?" His answer to that was "Yes, Grandma, I believe she does." Matthew's grandma stated that maybe this fact should matter more than the fact that I was nine years older.

Matthew told me that in those two days, God had given him peace to pursue a potential relationship with me. He agreed with his grandma that at our ages of thirty-four and forty-three, there were plenty of other issues that mattered more than age did at this point in our lives. I happened to agree.

Matthew asked Mr. Fry for my number on Wednesday evening and told him that he planned to call me after he got off work the next day.

# Chapter 8

Before going any further into the story, I want to insert that I am well aware that not everyone is meant to marry. Although I had definitely made *finding a husband* a matter of fervent prayer over the years, this was *not* something I prayed daily for. Marriage isn't guaranteed to everyone, and I knew that. I still remember my sister Amy being so confident that she would one day marry. I was amazed by this because I had never been that certain for myself. And by this time, although I was the oldest of three sisters, I was the only one yet unmarried. Amy had married in 1997 and Colleen in 2000. The year was now 2010. When I had informed my grandpa Walker about ten years prior that I had turned down Luke's proposition from North Dakota, my grandpa had turned away from me to look at my mother. He then said in a frustrated tone, "Kathy, she's never going to marry, is she?"

My dear faithful dad, however, never lost hope. Instead, he prayed daily for God to bring a wonderful godly man into my life. Year after year would go by, yet my dad never criticized my dating decisions, nor did he give up on God answering his prayer regarding me.

Through the years, I've come to believe strongly in being very specific with my prayers. I truly believe that we don't have any right to hope for things that we don't pray for. I also strongly believe that God often delights in answering *specific* requests, just because He *can*. So I have prayed in detail, and I've done it for many years.

When I would pray for a husband, I would start out by saying this: "Lord, if You *do* have a husband for me, would You please make it *so* 'crystal clear' that *I* cannot doubt, that *he* cannot doubt, and that those who love me cannot doubt that You sent him into my life." And besides praying that prayer, I kept a written list inside the front cover of my Bible, of qualities and traits that I hoped to find in a husband-to-be. By the time I met Matthew, that list had grown to fourteen different traits. I knew that the time had come for me to realize that *no* man could possibly check off all fourteen items on my wish list. Nonetheless, at the bottom of that list, I continued to write Bible references for promises God showed me in His Word that gave me reason to hope that He could answer this prayer for me.

Little did I know *then* that there would come a day when I would take that list out of my Bible and compare it to Matthew. On that day, a few months into my future, tears would blur my vision as I realized that God had found a man for me who fit each quality that I was hoping to find in a husband.

Well, on the very morning after I met Matthew Yount on that blind date of ours, I was turning in my Bible to find Psalm 12 (KJV). (At that point in time, I would read the chapter in Psalms and in Proverbs that coordinated with the day's date, and this was October 12.) But as I turned the pages, my eyes fell directly on Psalm 21:2, which states, "Thou hast given him his heart's desire, and hast not withholden the request of his lips." (Wow!) Then as I turned further, my eyes focused on these words in Psalm 34:10: "But they that seek the Lord shall not want (do without) any good thing." If I wasn't mistaken, it surely seemed as though the Lord Himself was speaking to my heart regarding a long-unanswered prayer request that I had brought before Him time and time again. It did not seem at all *coincidental* that my eyes fell on these verses when I was in fact looking for others...*and* on the very day after meeting a certain man named Matthew. For that reason, I decided to write the references down on a 3×5 card, date it, and tuck it in my Bible.

# Chapter 9

I had told myself not to *expect* a call from Matthew. Throughout the three days following our "date," however, people kept asking if I had heard from him yet. So of course, I began to hope more and more that I would.

For the first twenty-four hours after meeting Matthew, I was happier and more hopeful than I had been in many years. Then almost as though someone had flipped a light switch, I began to have very clearly formed conscious thoughts pop into my head. Questions were bombarding my mind, asking things like, "Why would you *ever* think that someone so much younger would be interested in you?" I was reminded, "You don't look like you used to." "You don't even know if you can still give a man children. It would be unfair to him." I realized that these thoughts were coming to me from the devil, not from my Lord…regardless of whether they were true or not.

On Wednesday night, two days after our blind date, I left a message on my parents' phone, asking my mom if she would call Mr. Fry. I wanted to find out what Matthew had thought of me. I told her that it felt unfair that Mr. Fry knew my thoughts about Matthew but I had no idea what Matthew thought of me. I also told my mom that I wanted to stop *hoping* if there was no point. If I needed to deal with disappointment, then I wanted to begin the process.

During the next two days, I would be at the school nearly round-the-clock since our school was hosting its annual volleyball tournament. My mom had planned to come out to the tourney on Thursday after she got off work. When she arrived at the school, she came directly to find me to give me her news from Mr. Fry. Dale had told my mother that he had been expecting her call. He mentioned that Matthew thought that I was attractive and easy to talk to. The reason he had needed to pray about calling me was due to the difference in our ages. (I can't express how excited I was that this very good-looking younger man found me to be attractive!) Matthew had told Mr. Fry that since God had given him definite peace, he planned to call me on Thursday evening.

I was ecstatic! And just then, I realized that *this* was Thursday evening! Let's just say that it didn't take me more than a few seconds to find my phone and to place it within my firm grasp.

And then he called!

My heart began to race as I quickly headed for the front door of the school, with phone in hand. Almost every square inch of Calvary Academy was packed with people on that day, and I had to find a place where I could sit quietly and talk. I answered the phone as soon as I stepped out of the building and into the sunshine. I started to walk toward my car as Matthew began to speak. Instantly, I became horribly distraught as I realized that every word I said to Matthew was echoing back through the phone into my ear. My phone had gone berserk, and this was *not* the time for that!

I explained the problem to Matthew and asked if I could hang up and call him right back. When I did so, the echoing problem only continued. There was no way I could possibly concentrate with this nonsense going on in my ear. I then asked if he would give me a few minutes to go back inside and borrow my sister's phone. After the situation was remedied, I sat in my car and we talked for an hour and a half!

Toward the end of the conversation, I explained that I wouldn't normally have Amy's phone nearby to borrow. For that reason, I asked if I could give him the number for my home phone in case my cell phone was to act up again. Then after realizing what I had just said, I interjected in an apologetic voice, "I'm sorry! You didn't ask if you could call me again. I shouldn't have assumed."

Matthew responded by saying, "That's okay! Yes, I want to call you again!" He went on to ask which day would be best for him to call. He mentioned that Friday, Saturday, or Sunday would work for him.

I repeated the word "Sunday" with a question in my tone because I was trying to determine how to explain my busy Sunday schedule to him. I simply said, "Sunday…um…?" and I hesitated.

In a quick moment, Matthew said, "Yeah, Sunday's too far away. I'll call you tomorrow."

I couldn't help but smile.

When I got home, I was eager to locate a leather journal that had been given to me as a gift from my sister one year before. I found it and decided to write down the details of what had transpired between Matthew and me within the four days since we had met. My opening line in that journal was: "Something tells me that I may wish to have this written down."

For this reason, you can be assured that most of the comments and the conversations you are reading about in this love story between Matthew and me are not only taken from the recesses of my very good memory. Most all of them were written down just after we had spoken on the phone or after we had spent time in one another's company.

During our very first phone conversation, I wanted to know if God was as real to Matthew as He is to me, so I asked him to tell me about the time that he accepted Christ as his Savior. Matthew wasn't the least bit offended but began to speak without hesitation. Matthew told me that he had been born again at the age of twenty. He had been a student at Edinboro University when a group of people who worked for the Gideons (the folks who put Bibles in motel rooms) had come to campus to hand out little New Testaments to the college students. Matthew had been a football player throughout his four years at Freedom Area High School and was six-foot-five-inches tall. He had an intimidating presence, as you can imagine; and he told me that he had not been in the mood to talk to these "missionaries" as he walked across campus. Matthew decided to reroute himself so that he would not walk directly past them, deliberately keeping his head down to avoid eye contact. Nonetheless, one gentleman caught up with him, pushed a New Testament into his hands, and said, "Son,

I know you have to be a very busy young man, but when you have the time, please read this little Bible. And when you do, pay close attention to the verses written inside the back cover. They tell you how you can know for sure that you are on your way to heaven one day." Matthew told the man that he would read it.

What the Gideon could not possibly have known was that Matthew loved to research and would read almost anything he could get his hands on. Matthew told me that he read this little Bible in three days' time. On Wednesday, October 16, 1996, after reading that New Testament from cover to cover, Matthew had a fraternity meeting which was housed in the campus library. After the meeting had ended, Matthew told me that he was not in the mood to socialize, nor was he ready to return to his dorm room. Instead, he got onto the elevator and found a floor in the library where he could be alone. Settling down into a chair, surrounded by shelves full of books, Matthew removed that little Bible from his pocket and turned again to read the verses written inside the back cover.

The words Matthew read explained that in order to know that we are on our way to heaven, we have to realize that Jesus Christ died on a cross for us. He said, "Becky, I was raised in the Lutheran church. I knew that already." He then read that we have to acknowledge the fact that we are sinners, in need of forgiveness. Matthew stated to me, "At that time in my life, no one needed to convince me of that. It was obvious." Finally, the little Bible said that there has to be a specific time in each person's life when we personally ask Christ to forgive our sins and to be our Savior. Matthew said, "*This* is what I had never done."

Matthew told me that there, inside the library at Edinboro University of Pennsylvania, he bowed his head and prayed to the God of heaven, confessing that he was a sinner and asking Christ to be his Savior. He picked up a pencil and wrote down his name and the date in the back of the New Testament. Matthew concluded this conversation with me by saying, "That was the best decision I ever made."

This account is also written in one of Matthew's journals, which I have beside me now as I write this for you to read. When Matthew began to journal about the day that he was born again, he began with these words: "I will remember this for the rest of my life…" (That little green New Testament, with Matthew's words penciled inside the back cover, is still kept in a drawer of my bedside table.)

Now it was time for me to share *my* testimony with *him*. I found it very interesting that both of us, as children, had gone to a Lutheran church. I told him that my family had been members of that denomination until I was about six years old. Around that time, my parents had gone to a Billy Graham crusade with a bus full of people. On the second night of the crusade, they mentioned to their friends that they wanted to go forward at the end of the service to talk to someone about being "saved." They asked that the bus wait for them. My parents, both in their thirties, were "born again" that very night.

Not many weeks later, my mom and dad asked to meet with their pastor in his office. They told him that they had gone to the crusade and that they had each made the choice to ask Christ to forgive their sins and to be their Savior. They then confronted their pastor by asking, "Why did you never tell us that we can *know* for sure that we will go to heaven?" The pastor replied that he was required to preach the sermons that were sent to him by the Lutheran Council of Churches, and that this was not included in those sermons. Shortly after the meeting, my parents began to search for a church that taught about salvation—not only about how to live a good life.

After visiting some different types of churches, my family settled for a few short years into a nondenominational church that preached the Gospel. It was there that *I* began hearing that Jesus loved me enough to die on a cross for me, and that if I were sincerely sorry for my sin, I could ask Christ to forgive me and to be my Savior. If I did this, I was shown that the Bible clearly states that we don't have to *hope* we'll go to heaven one day. We can *know* it.

Following the pastor's messages each Sunday in Homeacre Chapel, as this nondenominational church was named, the pastor would extend an "invitation" to come to the front of the auditorium. You were invited to come if you would like to ask Jesus to be your Savior…or if you would like to be baptized. For a number of weeks, I had begun to feel very uncomfortable during these "invitations."

Because I wanted to put an end to this feeling of conviction, I had decided that I was going to walk forward and talk to someone at the front of the church the very next time I felt this way. I would state that I wanted to be baptized. (My parents had had me baptized as a baby in the Lutheran church; but in this church, I would be baptized by immersion.) In my head, I reasoned that the guilty feeling might go away if I were immersed in water.

I can still remember the sun shining through the large stained-glass windows at the back of the church sanctuary on the Sunday morning that I stepped out into the aisle during the invitation and boldly walked forward. The pastor's wife put her arm around my shoulder and directed me to sit beside her on the front pew. She asked the reason I had come forward, and I told her that I wanted to be baptized. She told me that this was wonderful news and asked *when* it was that I had asked Jesus to save me. *This* question, I had never considered. But in my pride, I did not want *her* to know that she had caught me off guard. So I lied! I told the pastor's wife that I had asked Jesus to save me when I was little.

I was not baptized that day.

When I got home, I went to my bedroom; yet I could not stop thinking about the question that Mrs. Fisher had asked me. *I* knew there had never been a time when I had had a talk with God Himself and asked Him to forgive my sins. In *my* mind, I felt that I really hadn't ever given my parents much trouble. All in all, I was a pretty good kid. Anybody but my sisters would have vouched for me. (I think that siblings often know us better than most anyone else does.) Then I thought through all the things that I had been taught since attending this church. According to Bible verses that I had seen with my own eyes from God's Word, if I *could be* good enough to get myself to heaven, then it would have been *foolish* for God to have allowed His only Son to die a horrible death for me. I realized that maybe my sin didn't seem to be as awful as someone else's, but neither could I claim to be perfect. And that meant that I was a sinner who needed a Savior.

I explained to Matthew that I didn't need to find someone to talk to that day. I knew what I needed to do. I knelt down on my knees beside my bed and admitted to God that I was a sinner. I told Him that I was sorry that my sin had helped to send Jesus to the cross. I thanked Him for dying for me and asked Him to come into my heart to be my Savior. I believe I was ten years old. I remember the circumstances as though it happened yesterday. I just wish I had thought to write down the date, as Matthew had.

# Chapter 10

During Matthew's first phone call to me, he had mentioned being held up at gunpoint. This had taken place while he was working toward earning a master's degree at the University of Pittsburgh. Matthew explained that he had ridden the bus home from work as usual one night. As he walked the short distance from the bus stop to the carriage house that he and his cousin were renting, a man walked up to Matthew on the dimly lit sidewalk. The man directed his eyes to the handgun he was holding and demanded that Matthew empty his pockets. Matthew looked at him and said these very words: "Dude, you've got the wrong guy! I'm a grad student. I've got no money." The man insisted that Matthew empty the contents of his pockets onto the ground. He then told Matthew to turn around. Matthew told me that he remembered consciously thinking that he could have easily taken the guy, if it hadn't been for the gun. Matthew hesitantly turned around. The gun was then held to his back as the man sifted through his belongings. After deciding that nothing was worth taking, he told Matthew to start walking.

Matthew explained to me that he was so terribly shaken up after this that he went straight home and prayed. He told God that he knew beyond a doubt that he would have gone straight to heaven if the man had pulled the trigger that night because of asking Christ to be his Savior when he was twenty years old. He explained to me that in the few years since that time, however, he had gotten far away from living the way that he knew he should. He admitted that he often used language that was not appropriate for a Christian to use. Matthew also explained that he had allowed himself to become quite a drinker during his college days. He told me that the holdup had made him realize that he needed to "get it together" (as he worded it).

Matthew went on to tell me that at this same time in his life, he had been having a reoccurring dream that was particularly disturbing to him. This dream would begin with Matthew standing on the corner of a busy city street. He would then begin running as fast as he could down street after street as though he were running away from something. Then in his dream, he would feel himself being lifted up off the ground by the back of his shirt collar, only to be set down again at the very same spot where his dream had begun. After the holdup, Matthew began to feel that his dream was meant to show him that he could run as fast and as far as he wanted to run, away from his Savior. He now believed that God would always know where to find him and could always bring him back. After the holdup, Matthew made a conscious decision to conduct his life differently from that point forward. He decided that when he *did* get to heaven, he wanted to know that he had made his life count for something worthwhile and that he had lived in a way that was pleasing to his Lord.

Matthew was so sincere in this decision to surrender his life to the Lord that later, on our own wedding day, he would not even let the two of us drink punch from champagne glasses at our own "dry" reception. They had to specifically be "water goblets." Matthew explained that he wanted there to be no question in the minds of his family and friends that he had changed his ways.

Matthew and I talked on the phone four separate times in the next week and a half. During that fourth conversation, we spoke for three hours and forty minutes. The topic of "dating standards" had come up; and by this time, I was well aware that asking a guy to be willing to date as I had dated was a huge turnoff. In the past, this had been the subject that would often cause a guy to quickly bow out of my life. For this reason, I had prayed much concerning the issue before it came up in conversation with Matthew.

Our talk went something like this.

I wanted to know how it was that he ended up faithfully attending a Baptist church…the very same kind of independent fundamental Baptist church that my family became members of when I was twelve years old.

Matthew proceeded to fill me in. He told me that following the holdup, he once again began reading the Bible. In doing this, he quickly realized his need to get involved in a church; yet he had already tried so many of them. Matthew explained that he didn't have any direction as to what kind of church he should become part of; so in his frustration, Matthew called out to God again. Matthew told me that he had prayed, "God, it sure would be nice if You would just *send* someone to me, who could point me in the way You want me to go."

Only about a week or so after praying this prayer, Matthew explained that he was at his mother's home when a young missionary, who had been in the area speaking at Sylvania Hills Baptist Church, knocked on the door. I was told that Matthew's mom opened the door, heard what the man had to say, and then said, "My son might want to talk with you. Hang on." When Matthew arrived at the door, he had several questions to ask the missionary. After all questions had been satisfactorily answered, Matthew inquired as to when the next church service was being held. He was told that there was a service that very evening and Matthew went. He told me that he knew he *had* to go because God had so clearly sent this missionary to him such a short time after Matthew's prayer for direction.

After Matthew told me this story, he mentioned, "I've always liked to research things and study them out, you know. I hadn't done this with the Baptist church, however, and I really wish I knew more of its history."

I told him that I loved the history of the Baptist church and asked if he had ever read the little book called *The Trail of Blood* that I was required to read when I was a student at Massillon Baptist College. When he said that he hadn't heard of it, I responded by saying, "Well, if I get to see you again, I'll let you borrow mine."

He replied, "What do you mean, *if* I get to see you again?"

I answered, "Well, you've never said anything about that."

Matthew then took on a different tone of voice entirely and slowly spoke these words: "Okay…just so you know… I was talking to my best friend, Jeff Halliday, and I told him about you." He explained that he said to Jeff, "I really like this girl and I wonder if it's too soon to ask to see her again." Jeff asked, "Well, how long ago did you meet her?" Matthew answered, "I don't know…maybe two or three weeks ago." Jeff's recommendation was "Well, see how things go the next time you talk, and if it seems right, ask her out."

Matthew then said to me with a healthy dose of sarcasm in his voice, "*So*…since you *obviously* don't think it's too soon, would you go out with me again?"

I happily responded, "I would *love* to!" I added, "By the way, just so you know, it hasn't been two or three weeks since we met. As of today, we've only known each other for eleven days."

This line of talk turned out to be the perfect opening in which to discuss dating standards. So I took a deep breath and began. I said, "You know, with all the long conversations we've had, there is something we've never talked about that I think should be discussed before we see each other again."

Then my thoughts suddenly took an abrupt turn, and I did something I've *never* done before. I asked Matthew what *his* dating standards were. In all my dating years, I had never considered handling it this way. But I'm so grateful that God led me in that direction with Matthew.

When talking to other "romantic interests" in the past, I have always just simply stated the way I've always dated and planned to continue dating. Of *course*, I have never expected any guy to have dated the same way that *I* have. I strongly feel, however, that if a girl has a talk with a guy and discusses a line that she won't cross in a relationship, the guy will hold to it…*if* he cares enough about her. And if a guy isn't willing to respect a girl's wishes, it becomes obvious that he doesn't care enough about *her*. The fact becomes clear that he is in the relationship only for an agenda of his own. If no line is drawn and *verbalized*, I feel that it would surely become too difficult for one or both of them to hold back from what only comes naturally. This is why I have always covered the subject at the outset of a relationship.

And by the way, I'd like to mention a little-known fact. Dating, along with another couple (as I always did), does not need to be seen as a negative thing. Seeing how a guy (or a girl) interacts in the company of your family and friends will show you a whole different side of that person than you can possibly see when you only spend time *alone* with them.

Now I'll step down from my soapbox and return to my story.

Matthew hesitated after I completely and knowingly put him on the spot by asking what his dating standards were. Then he began by saying, "Well… I would like to date differently this time than I ever have before." He went on to say, "I don't plan to kiss, and I'm not real sure what I think about holding hands."

Well, not in a million years was I expecting Matthew to answer my question in such a way! What guy plans not to kiss…when he had not been taught as I had been taught? He then asked what *my* dating standards were. And I told him—all of them. Now, of course, Matthew had to find my dating habits to be very strange and unusual. Everybody did. So after explaining, I asked him the question that I didn't really want to hear the answer to. I asked, "Do you *still* want to see me again?"

There was a pause over the phone before Matthew replied. He spoke slowly and thoughtfully. "Maybe I should be the one asking *you* that question."

Confused, I asked, "What do you mean?"

He continued by saying, "Becky, I have dated quite a bit. I even had a serious girlfriend for a couple years who I thought I was going to propose to. I have *never* dated anything *like* the way you have. I *can* tell you that I let each of those girls know that there was a line I wouldn't cross until I married…but that's all I can say." After expounding on what he had inferred in that statement, he finished by saying, "So let me ask, do *you* still want to see *me* again?"

I replied, "Yes, I do." I went on to assure him, "Matthew, I only expected as much. Actually, what you just told me is better than I was thinking I might hear."

I wasn't naive and I've never been stupid. Matthew was a very good-looking thirty-four-year-old single man who had spent several years at two different public universities while earning his degrees. I knew that our dating relationships had been completely different.

Matthew grew quiet. Then he said these words to me: "I'm willing to date like that—if it means getting to know you better."

I was instantly glad that this talk was taking place over the phone so that Matthew couldn't see the large tears welling up in my eyes. As those tears began to fall, a slow smile began to stretch from ear to ear as I realized that I was going to get to see this man again. I could hardly believe it!

# Chapter 11

I had never before been one who enjoyed talking on the phone, but that immediately changed. Matthew and I lived about one hour apart. For that reason, an awful lot of our "getting to know each other" would need to take place over the phone. Right from the start, we were excited to find out that we both had the same cell phone carrier, which meant that there would be no charge for our calls back and forth. This would end up being a bigger blessing than one might think because we would end up talking on the phone for literally *several hundred* hours during the next ten months of time.

Matthew described himself to be a quiet, introverted kind of guy. It was a good thing that he told me this because over the phone, I would not have guessed it. We talked nonstop for hours at a time. (No, I'm not kidding…and no, I was not the one always doing the talking!) I truly cannot remember one single time that there was a lull in the conversation. There was so much that we wanted to know about each other, and we had both already lived through so many experiences that there was much to share.

On October 30, nineteen days after meeting for the first time, Matthew and I had our second date—or as he referred to it, our first "official" date. Matthew was not a fast-moving guy, but that was all right. I needed time to get to know what kind of man Matthew was on the *inside*. Sadly, it had always been entirely too easy for me to be overly critical and faultfinding with prospective guys when I spent time with them in person.

I wanted my sister Amy and my brother-in-law Aaron to be the first in my circle of family and friends to meet Matthew. I had asked Matthew to choose a place for this date that was close to where he lived since he had traveled to meet *me* the first time. The four of us met for dinner at an excellent restaurant called the Iron Bridge. Afterward, we walked around the Grove City outlet mall that was nearby so that we could spend more time together.

Although we had a nice time, both Matthew and I would have told you that there were no fireworks between us that evening. We both found each other to be attractive, but it is also true that there is much to be said for "chemistry." Matthew was very guarded and serious. And on the way home with Amy and Aaron, I was, as usual, very critical. I had always believed that I could only be with a fun-loving, easygoing guy who made me laugh. Matthew had been terribly serious throughout the evening as he had been on our blind date at the Frys' home. I had expected he would be more comfortable around me this second time.

Thankfully, my sister and brother-in-law provided the voice of reason that I needed to hear during the ride home. They reminded me that for nineteen days, all I could talk about was this great guy who I spoke with for hours at a time on the phone. They reminded me that Matthew and I shared so many of the same important spiritual beliefs. It was also pointed out that he was willing to date me in spite of my strict dating standards. I remember my brother-in-law specifically saying, "Becky, don't give up on this guy already. You're just getting to know him. Give it a real chance."

How grateful I will always be for the influence Amy and Aaron have had in my life!

Matthew and I continued our phone calls.

With each conversation, we were realizing that we had a great deal in common. Matthew and I found that we shared many of the same likes and dislikes, preferences, work ethics, character traits, political views, and even dreams. It was amazing. It was exciting!

Among other things, we discovered that we both had always been very close to our parents and grandparents. We both loved children and referred to them as "munchkins" and both used the odd phrase "all that jazz." We both favored dating brunettes (which I can tell you, *as* a brunette, does not seem to be a common male preference!) We both were extremely *appreciative* individuals. We both were very polite and had been taught great manners. We both loved history, but most especially Civil War history. Each of us held Abraham Lincoln as a hero.

We both loved college and counted those years to be some of our happiest. We each loved driving Hondas. I had previously owned two Honda Accords and he currently had a Honda CRV. Friendships meant much to us, both Matthew and I having friends whom we treasured. We each were very particular about things. We loved to have our belongings neat and organized. We were both a bit overly obsessed with toothbrushing. We both loved to travel, loved vegetables, and even specifically loved British accents.

We were astounded to realize that both Matthew and I had previously chosen Psalm 139 to be our favorite chapter of the Bible. We also discovered that just a few years before, we had each bought our living room furniture from the very same store in Butler, Pennsylvania. (Matthew had never been shopping in Butler before that time but came specifically to buy his furniture…less than five minutes away from where I lived.)

Slowly but surely, in spite of Matthew's serious exterior, I was able to see that sarcasm and dry witty humor ran rampant in both of our personalities. Matthew's sense of humor was definitely more "dry" than mine, to be sure. We also discovered that each of us enjoyed *instigating*. (He was the one to point out this fact.) But this, I must tell you, made our conversations very fun indeed!

On November 2, less than a month after meeting, we hit a rather large bump in the road. I was informed that Matthew considered two girls that he had met in college to be among his three closest friends in life. I believe he had known one of these girls for twelve years and the other for fourteen. Matthew told me that he shared especially close friendships with each of them. These friendships remained close through phone calls, placed once a week or thereabouts. I was told that he had been a wedding date for one of the girls in the recent past and that he attended an annual formal function with the other, year after year. Later, Matthew would reveal to me that the second friend had asked him to agree to marry her if both of them were still single by the age of forty.

There was no way I could pretend that Matthew's close connection with these two girls didn't make me tremendously uncomfortable. They were not just old friends. These were friends that continued to invest in each other, sharing and confiding on a regular basis with Matthew, in the most intimate of subjects, I discovered. Where it may not have bothered some, it posed a glaringly large red flag to me because of what I had gone through with Chad and Carla. It was instantly obvious that my heart still felt incredibly fragile.

I had no right whatsoever to ask that Matthew distance himself in these friendships—certainly not at this early stage in our relationship. I simply mentioned how uncomfortable it made me feel. I told Matthew in detail of the heartbreak I experienced in my last relationship, all because of what Chad and his female "friend" had been doing behind my back. I told him that while they were sharing this very inappropriate relationship, Chad kept telling me that Carla was only a very good friend and that he was trying to win *my* heart, not hers. Matthew felt that my concerns were unfounded and unnecessary when it came to him. At the end of this upsetting conversation, I explained to Matthew that I surely wanted to continue getting to know him. Yet if we were ever to become "serious" in this relationship of ours, these friendships would need to take a lesser position in his life.

Three days later, we again discussed the same touchy subject. This time, however, *I* brought it up and we handled ourselves in a much calmer and more controlled fashion. I mentioned the fact that, of course, I realized there is such a thing as a possessive, controlling kind of jealousy. But just as certainly, there is a *healthy* form of jealousy. I pointed out a particular verse in the Bible which states that God Himself is jealous over us, desiring our attention and devotion to be focused on Him. Matthew surprised me by saying that he had started looking for verses in the Bible on this subject and had read the very same verse. I reasoned that no new girl in Matthew's life could compete with two longtime female friends who continued actively investing in deeply rooted friendships with him.

At the beginning of our phone conversation the very next day, Matthew asked, "Well, do you want to know what I did today?" Following my response of "Yes, I do!" Matthew told me that of his own accord, he had called Tonilee, the friend he had attended a wedding with not very long before. He said that he gave her a "heads-up" in case his relationship with me became serious.

He was completely relieved when Tonilee responded, "Well… I knew this day would someday come. I am *so* happy for you, Matthew! I really hope that you and Becky work out. You just tell me what the boundaries are and I'll stick to them." Matthew said that she was completely supportive and understanding. She would later prove this to be true by traveling many miles to attend our wedding only nine months later. What a perfect example of true friendship!

The next day, Matthew planned to call the other girl, whom I will not mention by name. I'll just say that after shouting some angry words at Matthew, she hung up on him. He was hurt terribly by this response, even writing about it in his journal. A few months later, when we were planning our wedding, Matthew tried to speak with her again. That time, I was standing beside him as he left a voicemail for her, asking if the three of us could meet for lunch because he wanted to introduce her to me. She never responded to his offer and they never spoke again.

I cannot explain how surprised and touched I was that Matthew had made these two extremely difficult phone calls…and so soon. It made me realize that he was serious enough about me to invest fully in this new relationship between us. He was not holding back. And I decided that if *he* was willing to completely invest, then so was I!

During our phone conversation on November 15, I asked Matthew to promise that he would never call me because he felt obligated to but only because he wanted to. (I loved the fact that he liked to be the one to initiate the phone calls at this point in our relationship.) He promised. Then he went on to say, "Becky, the fact is I could talk to you all night. I really like you…and I can't wait to see you again."

One evening in early December, almost two months after we had begun dating, Matthew told me that his pastor had asked how things were going with us. Matthew explained that we were doing well but admitted that he felt very cautious and uptight when he was with me in person. Matthew explained to Pastor Barnhouse that he had been deeply hurt, a few years before, by a girl he expected he would marry. He explained that he did not want to be hurt again. His pastor reminded Matthew that I was not the girl from his past who had hurt him. He also mentioned that everything they both had heard about me had been good. The pastor ended by saying, "So don't miss out on what God may have for you because you're afraid of being hurt again."

We broached several uncomfortable topics as this particular evening's four-hour-and-forty-minute phone conversation continued. Matthew reminded me of a statement I had made to him the night before when I had said, "I think *I'm* more 'in this' than *you* are." Tonight, he wanted to talk about that statement. He began by saying, "I don't believe you're right about that!"

I said, "You don't?"

Matthew responded with "No way...no way. I like you. I want to be with you. I want to spend time with you."

I replied that I felt as though he had begun to drag his feet with us. Then Matthew explained again how badly he had been hurt before. He was simply afraid of being hurt again. He explained that he is an "all or nothing" kind of guy...black or white. He told me that his focus with us was on the end. Matthew admitted that this was why he was being extra cautious now. He said, "That's why I ask so many questions of you. I don't want to invest all this time if something is just going to break the deal later."

I replied, "That's exactly how *I* feel. I *completely* understand the reason for all the questions."

I told Matthew, as I had before, that I found it very hard to *read* him. This was challenging for me because ordinarily I considered myself to be able to read people very well. To be honest, I found Matthew to be an extremely *complex* individual. I said to him, "Let me be frank about something."

He replied, "All right, go ahead."

I then boldly spoke these words: "I don't *want* to be just another friend, pen pal, or someone you can talk with on the phone."

Matthew replied, "No way! You're not! I told you that I want to be with you. I want to hang out with you and get to know you better."

I told him that I, too, had been hurt badly in two different relationships. "But I want to tell you something about myself, Matthew," I began. "I am the kind of person who *cares* deeply, *loves* deeply, and yes, sometimes *hurts* deeply." I went on to say, "But that's okay because it's worth the risk. We only get to live this life once, and I want to live it fully."

I told Matthew that I was so deeply hurt over the Chad-and-Carla situation that I had asked God repeatedly to let me die. Matthew laughed and I became instantly offended. I said, "I'm not kidding!"

Matthew softly replied, "I know. I just can't believe you did that because I had prayed the same way after ending the relationship with the girl who had hurt me."

Matthew then pointed out that we had been speaking for four hours, but we both agreed that our conversation had definitely helped to clear things up. We continued talking for forty more minutes. During this last part of the night's conversation, I told Matthew that I wanted him to be assured that I had no intentions of "changing him." Although I believe this may happen sometimes in younger couples, I realized that at our ages of thirty-four and forty-three, we were certainly more established and set in our ways. I wanted him to know I realized that *what I see is what I'd get.* I expected Matthew to express *relief* at hearing this; but to my surprise, he grew quiet. Then he replied, "Becky, I don't think it should work that way at all. I don't believe that we are too old or set in our ways to work to change things for each other. If we care enough, we should be willing to do that." Once again, this man had amazed me.

During our talk on the evening of December 16, Matthew mentioned how tired he had been at work after we had talked for five hours and twenty minutes the night before. A lady who had spoken on the phone with him at work that day had asked if he had been out late partying the night before. He replied, "No, I talked with my girlfriend for five hours."

He told me not to be offended but that she had responded, "Well, please invite me to the wedding!"

Matthew asked me if *I* had told anyone about the length of that phone call. I told him that I had. I said that I had mentioned it to my good friend Karen who taught in the classroom beside me. Karen had raised her eyebrows and said, "If things continue like this, please let me do your wedding pictures!" I followed that statement by telling Matthew, "Now don't let that scare you."

Matthew replied, "I'm not scared! I told you that I don't date just to date. I date with that goal. That's what I'm aiming for."

On December 19, Matthew asked me if I took any razzing about the difference in our ages. I said, "No, I haven't. In fact, I think *I* have finally arrived at being fine with it, and *I* was the hardest to convince."

Matthew asked, "Why?"

I replied, "Because I think you deserve someone younger."

Then in a voice that sounded pained, Matthew said, "Oh! I didn't think you were going to say something like that!" He added, "There have been plenty of times that I think I don't deserve *you*."

# Chapter 12

By Christmastime of 2010, Matthew and I had known each other for two-and-a-half months. We had only seen each other five separate times but had spoken on the phone for nearly one hundred hours. We were excited that the holiday season would allow us the opportunity to see each other on four different occasions between Christmas Eve and New Year's Day.

Actually, when I invited Matthew to join me at my church for our New Year's Eve service, he had mentioned that he already had made other plans. Of course, this was a great disappointment to me, but at least he had agreed to join me on Christmas Eve for our candlelight service. During a phone call shortly before Christmas, Matthew was listing off the dates that we would see each other over the holidays. When he mentioned New Year's Eve, I said, "I thought you ditched me for that night!"

He apologized for that and said, "Well, I changed my mind. I want to start 2011…with *you*." I am quite sure that even my heart smiled upon hearing that comment.

I specifically remember asking myself on Christmas Eve if I had fallen in love with Matthew. Then after quickly realizing that I had to *contemplate* my answer to that question, I decided that I must not yet love him.

In only one more week I knew! By New Year's Eve, there was *no* doubt that I loved this man.

Just as assuredly, however, I had decided that I would *not* be the one to voice those words before he first said them to me. I did, nonetheless, want my feelings to be completely obvious to him. For this reason, I carefully planned what I wanted to say to Matthew at the end of the New Year's Eve service.

Only minutes after the official start of the year 2011, Matthew and I slowly walked out of the church building and into the chilly moonlit night. As we stood beside his vehicle in the parking lot, I looked up at Matthew and said, "I hope I get to kiss you on this night next year!" I knew that I shocked him, but I wanted to be certain that he understood. I wanted Matthew Yount to be my husband.

During our nightly phone call on January 2, Matthew told me that he appreciated what I said to him in the church parking lot on New Year's Eve. He then questioned, "That means we would have to be married before this kiss could happen, right?"

I smiled as I responded, "That's right."

He took a breath and said, "I definitely see that as doable."

I followed this up by saying, "Matthew, I should probably stop being 'forward' with you."

He responded by stating, "Well, maybe I haven't said things like that to *you* before, but I want you to know that I *am* always thinking ahead and looking forward to us." Matthew brought up something that my mother had said at the dinner table on New Year's Day. Mom had begun a sentence with these words: "If you two ever get married…" Matthew told me that his immediate thought was "What do you mean '*if*'? You could have just said '*when.*'" He went on to say, "Since I had not ever told you this, though, I didn't think you would want it said first in front of your whole family."

Matthew's next words made my heart beat even faster. He said, "I have no doubts about us." This statement completely shocked me because I was very aware that we had recently encountered a road-block which neither of us could see a way around. The conflict was realized a short while ago when we admitted to each other that neither of us wished to move to the other one's church. That admission had escalated into an argument; and since that time, the subject had been avoided.

So I questioned, "*No* doubts?"

He replied, "None."

I told him that I thought we still had one large unresolved issue; and that was whose church would become our home church should our relationship progress. I had previously mentioned to him that I would have an awfully hard time considering leaving my church. I had been a faithful member of Calvary Baptist Church for over thirty years since I was just twelve years old. The people there were like a large extended family to me. The academy where I had been teaching for twenty years was a ministry of that church. I was master teacher of a four- and five-year-old children's church class each Sunday and also "bus captain" of one of our church's Sunday school bus routes. All of my closest friends were also members of Calvary; and most especially, my parents, sister, brother-in-law, nephew, and niece attended all the services there as well.

At this point, Matthew had only been attending Slippery Rock Baptist Church for less than three years when he had moved to the area for work. Matthew had no family there. It is true that he had worked to become more active in ministries of his church; but he hadn't been established in full-time positions yet—other than singing in choir. He also had told me that he never had felt a need to become a member there. Multiple times, in fact, Matthew had explained that he deeply and genuinely missed his home church back in Rochester, Pennsylvania. It was just entirely too far away for him to make the commute back to Sylvania Hills Baptist Church. It had been there, under the teaching and preaching of Pastor Michael Bailey, where Matthew had first begun a deliberate surrendered walk with the Lord. Regardless, this was no easy decision. It was a subject that both of us had been talking much to the Lord about.

When I questioned Matthew further about this complicated situation, he said, "I'm not worried about that. It's not an issue anymore." Of course, I asked why it was no longer an issue. Matthew replied, "The more I pray about it, the more God gives me peace that He is leading me forward." He added, "I've even been wondering if perhaps I was only meant to be at my church long enough to meet you because otherwise our paths would never have crossed."

Upon hearing this, my eyes instantly filled with tears of gratitude for Matthew's understanding. Matthew then told me about a conversation that someone in his church had just had with him. This man had asked Matthew if I would be moving membership to his church soon. When Matthew told him that we were praying about whose church to make our home, Matthew was informed that the *girl* is always supposed to follow the *guy* in a choice such as this. Matthew's response was "Well see, I was thinking this decision was up to Becky and me." I was admittedly proud of Matthew for this candid reply and told him so.

Matthew then explained to me that he needed to pray some more about *when* to make this change. He did not want to rush things with joining my church because he did not want to rush things with our relationship. He mentioned that he felt all was moving along "perfectly" with us. I told him that this was wise and that there was no *need* to rush. I said, "Matthew, God will let you know when the time is right, if that's what He wants."

With a smile in his voice, Matthew replied, "That's something I love about this relationship! I love that we can talk about things and then pray for God's leading and watch Him work everything out."

On January 3, Matthew's mom received a thank you note that I had sent her for some homemade pierogies that she and Matthew's grandma had made for me. Matthew told me that he asked his mom to read the note to him over the phone. After reading it aloud, she asked, "I'm going to lose another son, aren't I?"

Matthew answered, "She's a keeper!"

When Matthew told me this, I asked him, "Did you mean that *I* am a keeper?"

He said, "*Yes*, you're a keeper! I'm going to keep *you*, if you don't mind."

During our phone conversation on January 4, Matthew explained that he was not going to call me the next day because of his heavy schedule but that he would talk with me again the day after.

I said, "Well, if you're not going to talk to me tomorrow, would you at least *think* about me that day?"

Matthew responded, "Oh, I think about you *all* the time…far more often than you would believe." Then he added, "I look forward to being able to hold you." (No one had ever said anything like that to me before and my heart skipped a beat.)

On the ninth of January, Matthew told me that four different people from his church had asked, "So when's the date?"

He answered, "We're not even engaged yet!" (I suppose I should make sure to mention that Matthew had not yet told me that he loved me!) Anyway, Matthew explained now that he had decided long ago to date a girl for two years before proposing. He then planned to have a one-year engagement. He told me in this conversation that he was not going to wait that long for us because we *knew* we were right for each other. I reminded him of my comment on New Year's Eve when I said that I hoped I would get to kiss him on that day *next* year. Matthew did not make me continue what I was preparing to ask. He interrupted and said, "That would be awesome!"

I interjected three words and asked, "By next year?"

He repeated the words, "That would be awesome!"

I reminded Matthew that I had always wanted to be head over heels in love with the man I would marry, and I told him that my heart was headed in that direction. I then said, "Before you act on what those four people suggested to you today, I hope you will make sure that *you* are head over heels too. Be 100 percent sure of it."

Matthew replied, "Okay, I can do that."

I believe you may be able to guess by now that I was extremely confused as to why Matthew had not yet told me that he loved me. I didn't need him to say that he was *in love* with me...just that he *loved* me. Time and time again, he expressed that he planned to marry me. I could not fathom why a person would plan to marry someone they didn't already love. He had even written a letter in which he told me that he was *certain* God had interceded in an amazing way so that we would meet. Why then did he not tell me that he loved me?

January 11 was our three-month anniversary. Both of us expressed that it seemed as though we had known each other much longer. That night on the phone, Matthew talked a lot about his job and how stressful it had become. Then he said, "I have a beautiful girlfriend, though, and there's a great church that I hope to become part of soon. So even if my work situation is stressful, two out of three isn't bad." Matthew had taken a framed picture of us to set on the desk in his office. He went on to say, "When I need the day to get better, I look at our picture and there you are, smiling at me."

I reminded him that if for no other reason, *I* was thankful that this job had brought him to Grove City, where he was living…so that we might eventually meet.

Matthew replied, "Every stressful workday would be worth it for that."

During our phone call on January 13, I told Matthew that I often have a thought that bothers me greatly. When he questioned me about this, I said, "Many times I think that you are too good to be true, and if I wait long enough, you are just going to fade out of my life."

He quickly denied this by saying, "No, I'm not going to fade out of your life." Then he asked, as an afterthought, "Do you *want* me to?"

I said in a forceful tone of voice, "No."

He replied, "Then I won't. I *want* to be part of your life."

I responded, "I want to be part of yours."

On January 19, Matthew gave me an insight into myself that I had never realized before. I had upset my mom that day and had started an argument without ever meaning to. I explained to Matthew that my sister Amy never seems to do this; but unfortunately, I am able to push my mom's buttons like no one else does. For some reason, I had expected Matthew to go to bat for my mom; but he did not. Instead, he said, "Well, you and Amy are very different." He went on to explain, "Amy is very calm and laid-back whereas you are more direct and straightforward. And some people can't handle that." Matthew said, "I know this because I am *also* direct and straightforward and I often upset people."

At the end of this talk, I said, "Matthew, I hadn't wanted you to know that I was upset tonight. About two minutes into our conversation, though, you figured it out and asked me what was wrong." I continued by saying, "Do you know what that means?"

He asked, "What does it mean?"

I said, "It means that you're learning to *read* people, and you told me that you've never been able to do that."

He grew quiet for a minute. Then he said, "Well, I want to be able to read *you*. I want to be able to tell when you've had a bad day or when something is bothering you. This is *good* then."

The next evening, on January 20, I was trying to make Matthew believe that I did yoga (which I have never even tried). When I nearly had him fooled, I laughed and said, "No, I don't do that! It's too much like exercise!"

He chuckled and exclaimed, "I *knew* we were perfect for each other!"

On January 22, we had been asking each other questions to determine how much we had learned about each other. Matthew told me that he had a hard question for me. Then he asked, "Is there anything about me that scares you?"

I grew quiet for a minute. I then began by saying, "You know, I always *expected* to doubt that a man was being honest with me."

Matthew interjected, "*I'm* honest!"

I replied, "I know." I added, "I also believed that it would be very difficult for me to *trust* that a man was who he claimed to be. I feared that I would always wonder if he was hiding something that he hoped I would never find out." I went on to reassure him by saying, "Matthew, you have been so transparent with me, telling me difficult things that you could have easily chosen to hide, and I never would have known. I have *complete* peace about you." I continued by saying, "The only thing that scares me is that you may never care for me more than you do now."

Matthew replied, "You do *not* need to worry about that. My family even knows that our relationship is going to be long-term, and they know how happy I am with you."

I said, "I'm glad to know that."

He said in a surprised tone, "You didn't know that?"

I replied, "Sometimes I wonder."

Matthew said, "Well, if you wonder again, you talk to me about it."

It was my turn to ask if anything about me scared *him*. Matthew quickly replied, "No, *you* specifically don't scare me. I don't have any concerns about *you*. My fear is that I won't be able to provide for you."

I asked, "Do you mean financially or spiritually?"

Matthew answered, "Financially…if I were ever to lose my job."

I assured him that God could take care of us no matter what the future holds. I then added, "I want to tell you something else. I knew it would be difficult for me to find someone who is as strong as I am spiritually. But, Matthew, your genuinely sincere walk with God allows me to have complete peace that I could rest in your leadership in my spiritual life."

He responded in a tone of appreciation with only one syllable, "Hmm."

This had been another four-hour conversation. At the end of it, Matthew asked, "Didn't your brother-in-law say that after we had dated a few times, our phone calls would shorten a lot?"

I answered, "Yes, he did."

Matthew responded, "Well, *he* was wrong!"

On the evening of January 28, 2011, I finally met Matthew's mom, dad, and grandma for the first time. I also met his aunt Sue and uncle Tony. This was the first that I saw Matthew's apartment as well. I had never been in an authentic "bachelor's pad" before, but Matthew's apartment was more nicely decorated than I would ever have imagined a single guy's place to be. When I mentioned this to him, he said, "The decorating was done by my mom and grandma. I asked them to help me out."

Matthew was the perfect gentleman that night. He had even bought my favorite kind of pop (which he always referred to as "soda") so that he would have it on hand when I came. He also insisted that I borrow his GPS so that I would not get lost going home in the dark.

I was incredibly nervous that evening, being well aware that I was making first impressions on people who I may one day be able to call my in-laws. Matthew assured me the next day that his family approved of me. His grandma had said, "I like her. I hope she liked us."

He replied, "Grandma, you have nothing to worry about!" He spoke accurately. Matthew has a great family that I am proud to be part of.

After I left, Matthew was asked if our dating standards would change when we got engaged. He had answered, "No, I don't think so." He later directed the question to me. Matthew asked, "Am I right about that?"

As the corners of my mouth lifted into a smile, I answered, "Yes, you are."

# Chapter 13

February had come. I had been having awful headaches for thirteen days straight. My blood pressure was extremely elevated, and I was unbelievably exhausted, having a hard time even functioning throughout my days. Instead of slowly getting better day by day, I was slowly feeling worse. I began to grow frightened that something inside me was very wrong. While at school one day, I became terribly dizzy and could barely keep myself awake. I knew that I needed medical attention, but I also knew that I could not drive myself to the hospital. My sister Amy picked me up from the school and took me to the emergency room. My mom met me there as well, and a few tests were run.

I refused to let the emergency room staff do all they wanted to do because I did not have medical insurance. For this reason, they were not able to find out what was really wrong. It was only determined that I had a severe tension headache and inflamed pressure points. I was given several intravenous fluids and allowed to fall asleep for a while in a darkened exam room. At one point, I remember seeing bright light spill into the room momentarily as the door was opened. The room darkened again as the door was pushed nearly shut. The ER doctor had come into my room.

He leaned against the wall and softly asked, "Rebecca, are you able to see me?"

When my eyes located him standing there in the dark, I groggily answered, "Yes."

Although I struggled to focus on what he was saying, I can recall the conversation still today. The doctor told me that he had been speaking to my mother in the hallway and that she had told him the cause for this "tension" that may likely have led to my continuing headaches. My mom had told him that I had fallen in love with a man who I had given up hoping I would ever meet. She told him that my whole family loved Matthew, but that he had never yet told me that he loved me.

This kind ER doctor said that he wanted to tell me something about himself. He began by saying, "After I divorced, there were several women who liked the idea of being married to a doctor." He went on to say, "Each of those women put a lot of pressure on me as we dated. Do you want to know who I finally fell for?"

I sleepily responded, "Who?"

His reply was "A lady who gave me all the time I needed…the one who didn't pressure me at all." He then finished by saying, "I am telling you this for a reason. If this gentleman of yours is as wonderful as it sounds like he is, then you wait for him. Give him all the time he needs."

I never would have thought that I would hear such needed advice from an emergency room doctor.

At a later date, my own doctor would order that a test for mononucleosis be done on me since I had not gotten well after a stretch of many weeks. By the time the test was run, it was shown through blood work that I was already in the convalescent stages of "mono." I had struggled through the illness, not missing one day of teaching. If you have ever had "mono" yourself, I believe you might agree that I deserved some kind of award for that!

On the night of February 10, after talking for a while on the phone, I said to Matthew, "Have you looked at the clock?"

He checked the time and said, "Do you know what I absolutely love about us? We can sit down and start to talk and somehow, the time just flies!" At the end of our phone call, Matthew said these words to me: "You're perfect for me, and I can't wait! I look forward to us. I think of holding your hand, holding you, stuff like that. I can't wait for that."

These sweet words surely perked me up. Because I was feeling so run-down, I asked Matthew for the first time if he would be willing to call me in the morning before work. I told him that I knew it would make me feel better to hear his voice. He kindly obliged and these short morning calls were added to our daily routine from that point on.

Matthew had accepted an invitation to join all of my family on a four-day mini-vacation to a rental home in West Virginia. There would be twelve of us. My youngest sister, Colleen, my brother-in-law, Larry, and my nephew and niece, Chase and Leanna, live in Tennessee. To help us stay connected, my family makes a trip similar to this almost every year. Never before had I brought a guy along on the trip, however. Matthew and I were looking forward to spending so much time together! I slept in a large bedroom with my four young nephews and nieces so that Matthew could have a room of his own.

Our time in West Virginia was wonderful. After the kids went to bed each night, Matthew and I joined my sisters and their husbands around the kitchen table for some old-fashioned board games until we could barely stay awake any longer. Throughout the long weekend, each couple took their turn making a meal for the rest of the family. Of course, Matthew and I had carefully planned ours. This was the first opportunity I was given to help Matthew make the recipe for his much-acclaimed homemade coconut cream pie, which was nothing short of *incredible*!

It's always hard to guess how "the new guy" is going to fit into an already made family, but Matthew fit like a glove! I was amazed by how well he got along with both of my brothers-in-law. It just felt like he belonged there with us…as though he was the missing piece to a long-unfinished puzzle.

After returning from our trip to West Virginia on Monday, February 21, Matthew and I were able to spend that upcoming Friday and Saturday together as well. Matthew had made arrangements for a special evening in Pittsburgh where he and I could enjoy a late Valentine's Day celebration together with Aaron and Amy. We had tickets to see Riverdance at the Benedum on Friday night, and he had chosen a nice restaurant for us to have dinner at beforehand. Matthew was invited to spend the night at Aaron and Amy's place afterward, and I would get to spend all day Saturday with him at their home.

After those two extremely enjoyable days were over, Matthew called to let me know that he had arrived back at his apartment in Grove City safely. It was Saturday evening, February 26. Matthew and I both expressed that we had had a great time being together that weekend. I then said, "There is a downside to seeing you so much though." (I had been with Matthew for six out of the last nine days.) I explained, "It just makes me want to see you more."

Matthew responded, "I know." Then he grew quiet.

After an uncomfortable length of time, I broke the silence by saying, "Uh-oh, you're quiet. I hope that feeling isn't one-sided!"

He sternly said, "*Becky*, it absolutely is *not!*" Then he hesitantly continued, "We should probably talk about this kind of thing in person."

I instantly became nervous and said, "I don't care if we're face-to-face or not. What is it that you would rather talk about in person?"

Matthew answered, "Well, then…how can I say this?" And all of a sudden, the tone of his voice became confident and deliberate as he said energetically, "You know, I'm just going to say it! I am *definitely* in love with you! I have been dying…*dying*…to tell you that for a week and a half!" He continued by saying, "I kept waiting for the perfect time to tell you. Then I would second-guess my timing, and I'd go home and beat myself up for missing my chance again. I wanted to say it in person." Then he added, "But I *will* say it in person, when I see you on Monday, when I talk to you on the phone, I'll tell you all the time that I love you."

My heart was racing as it never had before. I had thought that I just wanted to hear the three little words "I love you." Yet what had just come from Matthew's lips was so much more precious to me than what I thought I had wanted to hear.

I was finally ready to tell Matthew what I had felt for nearly two very long months. I spoke in a voice rich with emotion, "I love *you*."

He replied in a low soft-spoken voice, "Thank you."

Then the tone in Matthew's voice suddenly changed as he said, "I hope you won't be offended, but you are the *second* person I told."

I responded in confusion by asking, "I'm the *second* person?"

Then in a strongly apologetic and surprisingly loud voice, Matthew continued, "I told my FedEx guy!" I smiled while Matthew explained, "He always asks about us and this time he asked if I had proposed to you yet." Matthew said, "I told him I had not but that I am in love with you!" Matthew's FedEx man had been married for twenty-five years and had told Matthew that *his* marriage has lasted because of trust and communication. Matthew told him, "Becky and I have that! It's great!"

Matthew told me next, "I have *complete* peace about us. I have *no fear*, and I've never had that before with anyone! I've never felt any pressure in this relationship and I *love* that." This seemed to be the right time to tell him about the talk the ER doctor had had with me earlier that month. Matthew felt horrible that I had felt such stress without him realizing it. He told me something, however, that I was happy to hear. While I was being treated in the hospital that evening of February 7, Amy had been keeping contact with him by phone. Matthew told me that it was through the course of that evening that he realized how much he did not want to lose me. That was the night he said that he realized he loved me.

I said to Matthew, "I wish you could know how happy you just made me!" I went on to say, "I love that you didn't just say 'I love you' but that you're 'in love' with me." I told him, "That's what I wanted you to be."

Matthew responded, "I am *absolutely* in love with you! I can't stop thinking about you. I think about you all the time...all the time...all the time."

Before signing my name in my Valentine's Day card to Matthew only twelve days before, I had written, "Just so you know... I have fallen...head over heels." I now asked him, "Did you understand that I was in love with you without me using those exact words in your Valentine's Day card?"

He answered, "I have known that you love me, but not just because of those words. I could tell by the way you look at me and the things you do for me."

When I thought Matthew was about to end the phone call without saying "I love you," I said, "Hey, wait!"

As though he had read my mind, he quickly said, "I was *going* to tell you I love you before I hung up."

I said, "Well, I just realized that I don't need to wait for you to say it first anymore. I can tell *you*. *I love* you!"

Matthew softly replied, "Wow, my heart is racing! It is!"

We talked a bit more before ending the phone call when I asked, "Will you tell me one more time?"

Matthew said with much feeling in his voice, "I love you...*oh*, I love you!"

I had *never once* felt this way in forty-three years of life.

# Chapter 14

My sister Amy once told me that she had a feeling Matthew considered the words "I love you" to be a commitment. In a conversation with me one day, she said, "I'll bet he will wait until he is sure you are the one he wants to marry before he speaks those words to you."

"And if I'm right about that," she continued, "I would bet that after he *does* tell you he loves you, it will not take him long to ask you to marry him."

I didn't believe her, but she was right.

Two days later, on February 28, Matthew asked me what type of engagement ring I would like. He also told me that he wanted my parents to meet his mom and his grandma.

Matthew told me that he had talked to Nancy Fry the night of the twenty-seventh. (She was the lady responsible for telling my mother that she wished I could meet Matthew in the first place.) At his church service that evening, Nancy had asked Matthew, "How is Becky? How are you two doing?"

Matthew replied, "Really good! I'm in love with her." He told me that her eyes instantly welled up in tears as a smile spread across her face.

I ended our nightly phone call that evening by saying, "Matthew, *I* love…being *in* love…with *you*."

He replied, "I *like* that!" Then he added, "It's *great* to be in love!"

Matthew wanted to choose my engagement ring on his own; however, he wanted us to look at rings together so that he could know my taste. He explained that he wanted me to love the ring. Then he added, "But then when I *know*..." He paused and added, "How can I say this? It's not going to sound very romantic, but... when I know what I want... I want it! I'm ready! I'm not going to wait a year or two to propose. I love you! I'm ready!" At the end of our talk that evening, Matthew said, "I love you...oh, I love you!"

Just one week later, Matthew informed me that he wanted to ask my parents for their blessing on our future marriage. He planned to make the hour-long drive to my church on Sunday morning and join me for lunch at my parent's home afterward. Following church, I planned to deliberately stall by stopping for a while at my apartment to give Matthew time alone to speak with my parents at their house.

When I asked Matthew later what he had said to my parents, he replied, "I told them that I love you, that I would give my life for you, and that I wanted to grow old with you. I told them that we were planning to look at rings tomorrow, and I asked if I could have their blessing." My mom told Matthew that she and my dad had been praying for a man like him to come into my life for about twenty years. She told him that she had learned much from watching me through my ups and downs in life. Mom said that as she watched me remain faithful, she knew that God had to have someone very special for me. Dad and Mom *happily* gave Matthew their blessing.

After Matthew finished recounting the afternoon's events to me, he added, "I'm excited about our future!" He told me to expect to be seeing him a lot more often. Matthew had traveled to Butler on that Sunday. Then he would do it all over again on Monday, Wednesday, Thursday, and Saturday of that week. During our phone conversation the day before, Matthew had explained to me that saying "I love you" was a commitment to him. (Amy was right.) He told me that he would give his life for me because "that's what love is." He added, "If you were in a burning building, I would be in it too."

The very next day, Aaron and Amy traveled with Matthew and me to a large mall where we would look at rings. To give the two of us some time to do this on our own, my sister and brother-in-law went one direction in the mall while we headed the opposite way to find the nearest jewelry store. This "date" was simply to get an idea of what type of ring I wanted. Then Matthew planned to surprise me with a ring that he would choose himself from Garcia Jewelers in downtown Pittsburgh's Clark Building. After finding a couple rings that I really liked, we had Amy and Aaron meet up with us so that we could show them. Next, the four of us headed to a restaurant for dinner. I had learned that evening that Matthew would have chosen a ring that was very much my taste, even without my help. After realizing this, I said to him, "You have good taste!"

He smiled and smugly replied, "I have *great* taste!"

While talking on the phone the next day, Matthew told me that he hoped he wasn't making me feel rushed by wanting to get my engagement ring already. He explained, "It's just that I know what I want…and I want to be with you!"

That Saturday, we spent most of the day with my parents. Matthew patiently taught me how to play my first full game of chess. Then he and I sat at the dining room table and discussed possible wedding dates and honeymoon destinations. At the start of this conversation, I asked him, "Have you given any thought yet as to what season of the year you want to get married?" I explained, "If I know that much, I can start deciding on wedding colors."

Matthew looked directly at me and answered, "I would rather it be sooner than later."

The month was now March of 2011, so I said, "Well, if we married this fall on November 11, 2011, it sure would be easy to remember!"

Matthew said in a surprisingly disappointed tone, "Do you *really* want to wait until fall?"

I replied, "I didn't say that I wanted to wait until fall. I just wasn't sure what you were thinking."

Matthew then said very seriously, "I don't need an easy way to remember our wedding anniversary. I would like to marry this summer."

Well then, summer it was going to be! We asked my mom for a calendar and set the date for the twelfth of August. Matthew preferred sooner in the summer, but I had much to do to finish the school year, and I needed *time* to plan a wedding.

Later that evening, when Matthew realized how late it was, he looked at me and said, "I don't want to leave." I understood because I didn't want him to leave either.

I voiced concern to my mom and my sister Amy, saying that I didn't know how I could possibly plan a wedding in only a few short months. Please don't get me wrong. I was *absolutely* and *completely* excited, but this was the wedding I had hoped for all of my life; and I wanted it to be beautiful! I also am extremely particular about things. And even though I had *hoped* for my wedding day most all of my life, I had never allowed myself to mentally "plan" another wedding. (As a reminder, I had walked away from a wedding that didn't happen twenty-three years before, when I was engaged to marry Brandon.) For that reason, I was not like a lot of young women, who have already planned many of the details of their future weddings before they have even met their husbands-to-be. I didn't even know what color I wanted my bridesmaids to wear! But that was all right because I surely *did* know who I wanted to marry!

Mom and Amy told me that I would need to delegate some of the planning and responsibilities to them. Soon after, my mother-in-law (to-be) offered to help as well. Their kind offers, in large part, are the reasons I was able to remain mentally stable throughout the next few months while we planned a more beautiful wedding than I could have ever imagined.

At work that Monday, Matthew requested vacation days for August 12 through the next week for our honeymoon. Previously, Matthew had been invited to join Aaron and Amy's family and myself for a vacation at the Outer Banks of North Carolina in June… two months before our wedding. Amy was going to take our engagement pictures there on the beach. Now that he had taken time off for our wedding and a honeymoon, Matthew explained to me that he needed to shorten his time at the Outer Banks to only a few days so that he didn't use up all of his vacation time for the year. After strongly voicing my disappointment, Matthew said, "Think of it this way: just two months after that, it's you and me!"

I responded, "I know…but we won't be at the beach."

Matthew replied, "No, but I'll be waking up next to you!"

My heart melted. He couldn't have chosen a more perfect statement than that!

My parents were invited to Matthew's parents' home for dinner on March 19. This would be the first time they would meet. Matthew and I spent the early part of that day at my parents' home together. Shortly before we would be heading down to his folks' house, Matthew had closed his eyes for a short nap with his head leaned back against the couch. I decided to grab my purse, place it on my lap, and freshen my makeup while I sat beside him.

Matthew opened his eyes and said in a voice, not much louder than a whisper, "You're my pretty girl."

I thought he had been sleeping, so I asked, "Do you know what you just said?"

Matthew opened his eyes sleepily and responded, "I said, 'You're my pretty girl.'" When his eyes had closed once again, he added, "I can't wait till August."

I was so flattered! I replied, "Aww, thank you!"

Matthew once again opened his eyes and simply said these two words: "Can't wait." He then closed his eyes to sleep.

The next day was Sunday. Matthew came to my church for both the morning and evening services. Afterward, we had asked for a meeting with my pastor. Matthew told him that he wanted to join our church in two weeks and that we would like him to marry us on Friday, August 12, four months later. With a large smile on his face, Pastor Ward happily agreed to officiate in our wedding and told us to have his secretary put the date on the calendar right away. After agreeing to meet several times throughout the upcoming months for premarital counseling, we thanked him and walked out of his office. In only moments, Pastor Ward pulled us back inside to explain to Matthew his purpose in asking for weddings to be done on Fridays as we had chosen. Then Pastor Ward said, "I would not refuse to marry you on a Saturday, however, if that's what you really wanted."

I looked up at Matthew and asked, "Are you still good with a Friday wedding?"

His face softened into a smile as he tenderly looked down at me and answered, "*Yes*! I would marry you any day of the week!"

On April 1, Matthew spoke these words to me over the phone: "I prayed a long time for you. I can't *wait* to spend the rest of my life with you." Two days later, he said, "August can't come soon enough. Will you marry me next week?" Matthew had told me that he didn't consider himself to be very romantic, but I believe he was absolutely wrong about that. I *loved* how he would speak whatever he was thinking.

*Engagement pictures taken by my sister Amy at the Outer Banks in North Carolina*

*My dream came true!*
*August 12, 2011*

*Our beautiful wedding ceremony*

*Matthew and I with our eight nephews and nieces*

*The day I married my prince charming!*

*Matthew and Becky with our parents*

*Becky's sisters and their families*

*Matthew's brother and his family*

*The happiest day*
*of our lives*

*Heading to the Bahamas on our honeymoon!*
*Alone together at last.*

*My favorite place to*
*be—in his arms*

*Our second wedding*
*anniversary*

# Chapter 15

Monday, April 4, 2011, started out like any ordinary Monday morning. Sometime early in the day, however, everything changed. Someone knocked on my classroom door then opened it to tell me that I had a delivery. I was handed a vase holding two beautiful red roses and daisies. Matthew had the bouquet delivered to the school with a simple note that read, "Just thinking of you." Now that was sweet!

I'm sure you can imagine my surprise when the very same thing happened the next day, as an identical bouquet was delivered along with a note. This one read, "I am so glad we met." The second bouquet drew even more attention and curiosity than the first one had, I must say!

But it happened again on Wednesday, on Thursday, and on Friday! On these days, high school girls and guys were stopping me in the hallway to ask if I had gotten more flowers from Matthew. Often they would step into my classroom during break times and ask if they could read the notes. On the last three note cards were written these words: "Looking forward to us," "You are my love," and "Together forever." All of the students were excited for their former third- and fourth-grade teacher and couldn't help but be impressed with her boyfriend. One of my fourth-grade boys, however, found the flower deliveries to be rather irritating. At the end of the week, when I walked into the classroom with another bouquet, he looked up from his desk. In a loud and annoyed voice, he called out, "Flowers *again*?"

It is true that I am a hopeless romantic and I was completely smitten! I felt I was in the middle of my very own fairy tale.

Before the week had begun, Matthew had said that he would like to take me out to dinner that Saturday. We would be going to a nice restaurant, but he would not tell me where. Matthew had prepared me that this would be a dress-up occasion, and that he, Amy, and Aaron would be picking me up at my apartment. This was unusual because we would often drive separately and meet at our destination.

I was to be ready at three thirty in the afternoon on that Saturday, April 9. Matthew was an incredibly punctual man. Because of that, I had previously asked him if he wanted me to be ready to walk out to the car when he arrived. I suggested that maybe he would like to come inside first to see the five bouquets of flowers that he had had delivered to me throughout the week. Matthew told me that he would like to come in and see them when he arrived.

At three thirty, there was a knock on my door. When I opened it, Matthew was standing on my doorstep with one hand behind his back, looking as handsome as ever. He was wearing khaki dress pants, a navy sport coat, light-blue shirt, and a burgundy striped tie. As I moved aside, making room for him to enter, I said, "Come in and see the beautiful flowers you sent me!"

Matthew pulled from behind his back one more matching bouquet of flowers and handed it to me as he stepped inside. He said, "Now you have a total of twelve red roses. I had decided a long time ago that I would never buy a full dozen roses for any girl until I was sure she was going to become my wife." (Amy and Aaron were waiting for us in the car and had secretly snapped a picture of Matthew at my door with those roses behind his back.)

Matthew walked through the kitchen and entered my living room where the flowers were all lined up in a row on my computer desk. He absentmindedly looked at them, commented briefly, and then turned around. Because we were planning to leave, I had turned all the lights off before Matthew came. This was the middle of a sunny afternoon, and my apartment was full of windows, so the room was flooded with natural light anyway. Yet still, Matthew walked over to a light switch on the wall and flipped it on. Then his feet stood frozen in the middle of my living room while he reached into the inside pocket of his sport coat. Matthew's eyes never left mine as he pulled out a ring box. As he did this, Matthew began to speak these words that I attempted to memorize: "Becky, there isn't a day that goes by that I don't think of you. You are on my mind *all* the time. You are absolutely wonderful, godly, beautiful." Then he choked up and I could see tears in his eyes. I can still clearly picture the scene as Matthew placed his hand on his chest. Then he said, "I would be *honored* if you would be my wife." He lowered his tall frame to one knee. After Matthew had opened the box to remove the ring, he held it out to me and asked the words I had desperately wanted to hear, "Will you marry me?" His voice lifted on the last two words, making it sound as though he was not sure of the answer I would give.

I spoke the words I had rehearsed in my head time and time again, "Oh, absolutely yes! I have waited for you all of my life."

As Matthew placed a stunning princess-cut diamond engagement ring on my finger, his hands were horribly shaking. After the ring was in place and I held my hand under the light, I realized that my hands were trembling too. I asked why his hands were shaking so badly when he had to know that I couldn't *wait* to say "yes." He claimed that he was not sure I would like the ring he had chosen. But it was perfect! Matthew asked, "Would you like to know where we're going to eat?"

I quickly replied, "Yes!" He had made arrangements to take me to an elegant restaurant called Shakespeare's, which sits on a golf course and was built to resemble a castle, surrounded by a large stone wall.

Amy and Aaron had planned to be seated separately, far across the large dining room from where Matthew and I were taken to sit. That was the first time I had ever sat alone with a man at a restaurant, and it was wonderful—perfectly cozy and intimate! Over dinner, Matthew stated that he remembered the first time he met me. I asked if he remembered what his first thoughts were, and he said, "Yes! I thought, 'Wow! She's really beautiful! How can she possibly still be single?'"

After thanking him for those sweet words, I said that my immediate thought upon meeting *him* was "He is *really* good-looking—not at *all* what I expected!" My second thought was "Wow! Is he ever tall!"

While still at the table in Shakespeare's castle, Matthew asked, "Does the ring feel right?"

I smiled, looked across the table at him, and softly said, "It feels just right. *All* of this feels very right."

Days later, one of Matthew's work acquaintances heard that Matthew and I were engaged to marry after only six months of knowing each other. Instead of offering his congratulations, the man immediately gave Matthew a stern lecture. Matthew was told that he had better find out what my finances were like because it was very possible that I was hiding debt and bad spending habits from him. "Six months is not long enough for two adult people to know all they need to know about each other," my fiancé was told. Matthew explained to me that he quickly countered back, "Becky and I have *great* communication! She and I have already sat down together with lists of our income, bills, and budgets. I cannot imagine anything important that we have not already discussed."

During the first week of May, Matthew sent me a beautifully romantic letter, which was totally unexpected. I enjoyed it so much that I decided to surprise *him* with the most romantic letter I had ever written. Matthew called after receiving my letter and told me that he loved the part where I wrote, "I cannot wait till we're married and I can take your hand in mine or kiss you anytime I want to." He explained, "That's exactly how *I* feel. I can't wait to hold your hand, to kiss you, and all of that. I can't wait to be with you." I told him that my dating standards were harder for me to keep than they *ever* were with anyone else. That surprised Matthew. In the next breath, though, he shocked me by stating, "I think it might be easier for me."

When I asked why, Matthew responded, "Because of this. You have been completely 100 percent faithful—in not holding hands, kissing, or anything…up till now. I *will not* be the one who causes you not to make it to the altar that way. I will not tempt you in any way. We're gonna do this, Becky!"

After spending time together at my parents' home late one night shortly after that conversation, Matthew and I walked together toward our cars before heading to our respective apartments. We stood behind one of our vehicles to say goodnight. When I looked up at my fiancé under the moonlit sky, I asked, "Matthew, would you please just give me a hug? That's all I want."

My jaw nearly dropped to the ground when Matthew softly answered, "No."

In an unintentionally exasperated tone of voice, I responded, "What?"

Then he gently replied, "Becky, remember that I have never dated like this before meeting you, and I can tell you for a fact that when a guy hugs a girl that he loves, it changes things for him." I watched then as a mischievous smile began to spread across Matthew's face. Then he added, "But I can *also* tell you that we are *so* gonna make up for this after we're married!"

I couldn't help but smile too.

I'm not sure I have ever personally known a man, other than my Matthew, who possessed this kind of integrity.

By the middle of May, most of the major wedding-related necessities had been taken care of. During our nightly phone call on May 14, I said to Matthew, "I find more things that I love about you all the time." We ended our talk by reading together a chapter out of the book of Psalms and praying. After he prayed, I stayed quiet because I was crying.

Matthew asked, "Is something wrong?"

I answered, "Nothing's wrong. I just feel very blessed."

He asked, "Why?"

And I said, "Because of you."

Matthew responded with a half-laugh and a smile in his voice, but he spoke no words. I only heard the sound "Hmm" on my end of the phone. I finished by saying, "Thank you for being my fiancé. I can't believe I get to marry you!"

Matthew replied, "*You* can't believe it? You've got to be kidding! I can't believe I get to marry *you!*"

Everything you have read about in our fairytale-like romance up to this point had been written down in either my notes or in Matthew's journal. Because I have no further sweet conversations chronicled on paper, I will quickly proceed to our wedding day.

# Chapter 16

M atthew and I had chosen the theme "Dreams Do Come True" for our wedding, borrowing it from the wedding invitations that my sister had found for us, picturing a castle at the top of a winding hill.

As near as we were able to calculate, approximately three hundred family and friends were present at our wedding. I do not believe I had ever seen Calvary Baptist Church as full as it was that day. We had even rented additional chairs with the goal of seating as many guests as the auditorium could hold.

Between the two of us, Matthew and I had eight nephews and nieces whose ages, at the time, ranged from two to ten. We included all of them in our wedding party. We had asked each of our siblings to stand for us as well as several longtime friends who had been with us through all of life's major twists and turns. What a wonderful group of people stood on the platform with us that day!

All of my closest friends and fellow teachers were involved in one capacity or another to help make our wedding day all I had ever hoped it would be. My most recent students, along with a large number of former students (and parents of those students), added to our happiness as well. Matthew and I both had many precious friends—some even from years gone by—who traveled many miles to share in our wedding celebration. We each were deeply touched to see how many of our family members had made it a priority to be present to share with us on our special day. For many, this involved taking time off work for a weekday wedding and arranging to travel across several states to join us in Pennsylvania. I had never before felt so loved by so many.

Friday, August 12, 2011, was truly the happiest day of my entire life! Throughout our engagement, I had been praying for beautiful weather for our wedding day; and even *that* prayer was granted. The day was sunny and gorgeous! Matthew and I were surrounded by the love and well-wishes of the people closest to us on this earth. And *I* got to marry my very own "prince charming"! Matthew had turned thirty-five at the end of July; and I had turned forty-four, only six days before our wedding. Strangely, however, my age no longer seemed to matter so much. All those years I had been single seemed now to be oddly insignificant. I was truly and completely head over heels in love with the man who had just committed to love me for the rest of his life.

The day following our wedding, we would be flying to Miami. Then on Monday, we would leave on a honeymoon cruise to the Bahamas. We would be traveling, just the two of us—for the very first time!

Leading up to our wedding day, Matthew had prepared me, time and time again, that he would not be using his cell phone on our honeymoon. He always followed that statement by saying, "This honeymoon is all about *you* and *me*!" He had explained in no uncertain terms that his phone would be turned off with only two exceptions. First, he would call his mom to let her know that our plane had arrived in Miami safely on Saturday afternoon. Lastly, he would call her at the end of the week to let her know that we had gotten off our cruise ship safely and were back in the United States. He would not read or send one text message for the duration of our honeymoon. I loved this decision and followed his lead completely, only contacting my family when he contacted his.

If you stop to think about it, today's tech-savvy society doesn't typically "unplug" for much of anything. Although it is not pleasant to admit, often we are much too easily distracted by our cell phones. For all the good they do, it is still an unfortunate fact that sometimes our phones make it difficult to fully concentrate on the person in front of us desiring our attention. Matthew was making a deliberate choice to place his focus solely on me for the duration of our eight-day honeymoon trip. There was something completely endearing about that. Right from the start, my husband had an unmistakable way of making me feel cherished.

# Chapter 17

Shortly before we married, Matthew had said to me, "I sure hope you're going to be affectionate! *I need* that."

My answer had been: "Well, I have no frame of reference, but I think I might be."

He responded, "I *hope* so!"

I have to say that I surprised even myself. Showing affection came more naturally and easily to me than I ever dreamed it would. But I'm also sure that this had much to do with my openly affectionate husband.

Matthew and I walked hand in hand almost everywhere we went. We held hands while walking across parking lots, through malls, and even while walking the track at a nearby athletic field or throughout our neighborhood for exercise. If Matthew had started out ahead of me, he would continue to walk while facing forward. At the same time, he would stretch one arm out behind him with his hand open, waiting to grasp mine. Without speaking, this action meant "Hurry and catch up." Our hand-holding was usually initiated by Matthew, yet I cannot explain how much I loved it.

There is something I find precious about watching a couple holding hands while walking together. My grandpa and grandma Walker had done that for as long as I can remember, and I have always treasured that memory of them. If you give it some thought...*any* man and woman can be seen walking together someplace. However, when that couple is seen holding hands, any possible question about their relationship to each other is erased; and automatically, you assume that they must be in love. I had lived so much of my life single and alone. I *loved* the fact that it was even clear to perfect strangers that Matthew and I were a couple in love.

Before returning from our honeymoon, we had a conversation during which we agreed to never leave each other without a quick kiss goodbye, no matter how many people were around. Never one time was there an exception to this arrangement. Even if I had not initially requested this, Matthew had written in his journal about the subject long before. In that journal, he explained that when he had a wife one day, he planned to always kiss her goodbye when both were heading in separate directions. The reason was simply, as he worded it, "You never know when that goodbye may be the last." As a rule, we also ended phone calls and text messages to each other with the words "love you."

The first Monday following our return from the honeymoon, I got up early to see Matthew off to work...as I would continue to do every workday thereafter. I washed my face and brushed my teeth. Then I joined Matthew as he walked to the door. We both stopped and I lifted my face to kiss him goodbye before he left the house. Matthew leaned down, placed an arm around me, and gave me a nice little peck on the lips. Still looking up at him, I vividly remember asking in a disappointed tone, "So that's *it?*" Matthew did not respond verbally. Instead, he leaned down once more, placed both arms around me this time, and kissed me slowly and passionately. That second kiss took my breath away. I kid you not when I say that every workday after that, we shared a beautiful morning kiss. Most often, they were brief yet *always* romantic. Never again did I get a quick little peck, as he was heading off to work in the mornings. Every now and then following one of those kisses, however, Matthew would say, "You know you're spoiled, don't you?"

I always replied, "Yes, I do...and thank you for spoiling me." Then he would smile as he opened the door to leave.

Before we married, Matthew had told me that we were going to make a conscious ongoing effort to keep our love alive and to keep it growing. "Date nights" would be a part of that. I recall Matthew saying to me, as we neared our wedding date, "I cannot *wait* to go on dates after we're married!"

I was confused and said, "We go on dates *now*!"

He explained, "Yes, but we never go anywhere by ourselves. *That* will soon be changing!" We discussed the fact that neither of us wanted to become a divorce statistic one day, and we were completely aware that far too many couples fall *out* of love. We realized that marriage takes two, and there were two of us who agreed wholeheartedly to invest in our relationship on a regular basis. We made a decision to never take for granted the remarkably special love that God had blessed us with.

I distinctly recall a lesson I learned on our very first date night after marriage. I cannot remember exactly where we were going. I can, however, still picture the stretch of highway we were driving along as I sat in the passenger seat while Matthew drove. I was texting my sister on my phone when I heard Matthew speak four words in a sad tone of voice. "I can't believe it" was all he said.

I asked, "What's wrong?"

Matthew explained, "After ten months of dating you, I finally have you all to myself on a date…and you're talking to someone else on your phone."

I explained, "It's just my sister."

He said, "It doesn't matter *who* it is."

I put my phone away and did not pick it up again that evening.

I learned a lesson that night that I never forgot: quality time was extremely important to my husband. When we went out on a "date," that segment of time was just for the two of us. We owed each other our undivided attention.

I also remember both of us noticing couple after couple, sitting together in restaurants, yet seldom speaking a word to each other. We would see them completely involved with their phones, watching other people, or staring out the window as they ate. It was surprising to watch how long couples would sit, eating dinner together in complete silence. We vowed to never allow that to happen to us.

I will admit that I broke this promise once when Matthew took me to a special restaurant in Pittsburgh. Although this was a date that both of us had especially been looking forward to, I had gotten upset about something on our drive to dinner, and I was the one who had nothing to say to *him* at the table. Matthew looked up at me after several long minutes and said, "Now we're one of those couples we said we would never become. Let's *get past it* and enjoy being here together."

I adjusted my attitude and we enjoyed our meals *and* each other's company.

Because our love was a gift from God, Matthew and I made another conscious choice from the very beginning, to make God the Head of our home. We had established a time when we would read the Bible and pray together as a couple. We read a devotional book especially for married couples as well. We also faithfully and consistently attended church services together. I am confident that this was the main key to our happiness.

For several months after Matthew and I returned from our honeymoon, my dad would regularly walk over to us at the end of a church service. He would look directly at my new husband and ask, "Well, Matthew, is the honeymoon over yet?"

Matthew would emphatically respond, "*No*, it's not over yet!"

As he said this, Matthew would unfailingly turn to face me, wrap me up in his arms, and hug me tightly to him. Thanks to my dad's teasing, I received many tight embraces from my husband right at church!

# Chapter 18

Matthew and I had been told once before marriage that we were likely to have some knockdown, drag-out fights after we "tied the knot." Upon hearing this statement, we both had been instantly offended and quickly asked the reason why. We were given this answer: "You two are such strong-willed and opinionated individuals! You have each lived alone for a long time, and you're used to having things done your way. While you're dating, you both are on your best behavior! But after the honeymoon…you'll see!"

Well, if I remember correctly, it was two or three months into marriage when I asked Matthew, "Hey! Do you realize how well we are adjusting to married life?" When I had started to ask that question, Matthew had already begun to walk away from me, heading out of our kitchen and toward our living room. He stopped in his tracks and turned to face me. With a large grin on his face, my husband slowly and emphatically responded, "*YES, WE ARE*!" He began to walk away again but instead stopped and turned around once more. Then Matthew added, "But you know what? The Creator of this universe hooked you and me up. It was *bound* to be good!" He then smiled sweetly at me and walked away.

So many times at the beginning of our marriage, I would hear Matthew call out to me, "Hey!" The word was always pronounced real quick and real short. At first, I assumed he wanted to ask me something, so I would look at him and respond, "What?" Matthew never had anything to say though. He would just look at me and smile. In a short time, I came to understand that Matthew was only saying "Hey!" to me for one reason: he was simply acknowledging my presence to let me know that he was glad I was there.

The school where I was teaching is a ministry of our church, and both church and school are in the same building. That means that the school classrooms double as Sunday school classrooms every weekend. Because of this, the members of the church are on a cleaning rotation to get those rooms set back up for Monday's classes. (There is a reason for me telling you this.) Matthew and I would take our turn for three months out of the year; and Matthew made even this more fun for me. At some point, each time we were cleaning our assigned classroom, Matthew would stop what he was doing... whether he was moving chairs and desks into place, sweeping the floor, or cleaning off the whiteboards. He would stop abruptly, walk slowly over to where I was cleaning, and wrap his arms around me. He wouldn't say a word. He would simply hug me or kiss me and then return to the work he had been doing. The classroom door was always open, which means that anybody who happened to walk down the hallway at one of those particular moments could have seen his show of affection. Matthew didn't care and I loved that.

As I have already mentioned, my husband and I would always hold hands while walking together. Of course, this included our walk down the long flight of steps that leads from our church auditorium to the parking lot. But every so often, at the bottom step, he would release my hand and say, "Wait a minute!" Then he would jump down off the bottom step and turn to face me. Matthew would wrap his arms around my waist and sometimes say, "*Now*, you're on *my* level!" (Remember, he was 6'5" tall.) He would kiss me and then lift my 5'6" frame down beside him. This did not only happen right after our honeymoon. It continued to happen throughout our marriage.

At home, Matthew always looked for opportunities to find me on steps. Whether he saw me walking up a few stairs or standing on a stepladder to reach things in our kitchen cabinets, I could usually expect to find him waiting with a ready kiss when I turned to come down.

This husband of mine regularly walked up close behind me at home. He would enfold me in his arms, rest the side of his face against the top of my head, and just hold me for a couple minutes that way. I might be cooking at the stove, washing dishes, or any such thing. I came to expect this at some point every single day. Matthew told me that holding me in his arms this way was one of the things he loved most in our marriage.

The following memory will forever be one of my favorites. Matthew and I did not have central air-conditioning in our apartment. We used two window air conditioners and a couple fans. One of those air conditioners was very large and heavy. Instead of removing it from the window every fall, we would cover it from the outside with heavy plastic to protect it in the winter. Then we would seal it around the edges with duct tape to prevent cold air from blowing in. Well, the third and final time we completed this project together, Matthew had finished taping the plastic to the outside of the window frame. But being the perfectionist that I regrettably admit I am, I asked if I could climb the stepladder to inspect his handiwork. Instead of getting angry and offended, as many men may have, Matthew smiled slightly, stepped aside, and allowed me to climb the stepladder. While I was standing higher than he was for a change, Matthew stood behind me and gently wrapped his arms around my legs, lovingly resting the side of his face against the small of my back. He just held me like that until I was ready to come down. Our house is in the city, which means that neighbors could certainly have seen him; but that didn't matter to my Matthew.

There were times, at night, as we lay side by side in bed, when Matthew would unexpectedly rise on one elbow and begin to trace the contours of my face with his fingertips. In a soft-spoken and tender voice, for long moments of time, Matthew would tell me how much he loved me as his fingers gently traced over my face.

To be honest, I always thought that marriage could be *good*, but I never expected it to be *great*. *Our* marriage was surprisingly and amazingly *wonderful!* Matthew himself told me that often he would be asked, "So, Matthew, how is married life treating you?"

He would come home and tell me that his consistent reply was "Married life is *great!*"

# Chapter 19

I cannot tell you that Matthew and I never quarreled or argued because that would be entirely untrue. I *can* tell you, however, that we both knew how to communicate very well; and we knew how to compromise. We also realized the importance of knowing how to forgive and make up.

Both Matthew and I worked Mondays through Fridays only. Neither of us had jobs that required us to work evenings or weekends. This fact, in itself, was a huge contribution to helping the two of us develop an incredibly close marriage relationship. We did almost everything together.

For as long as I can remember, I have lived an extremely busy life. Matthew was not used to that. As a single man, he told me that he often had a lot of downtime, which he enjoyed and even needed. After marriage, Matthew didn't have much time alone at all; and sometimes, I felt very guilty about that. One day, this topic had come up again in conversation; and I suggested to Matthew that perhaps he could stay home and let me do the grocery shopping alone. Matthew considered this only for a brief moment before answering, "I'm going to say 'no' for two reasons. The first reason is because I love food [and he smiled]. The second reason is because of this." He then recounted for me one of his childhood memories. Matthew recalled being a boy of about eleven or twelve when he was in a check-out line with both of his parents. He said that the cashier was a lady they saw at that store regularly. She looked at his parents and said in a surprised tone of voice, "Hey! I never knew you two were a couple! I have never seen you together until today!" Matthew explained to me that he made a conscious decision at that moment, all those years before. He said to me, "I decided that one day when *I* was married, I was going to be seen together with my wife on a regular basis and everybody was going to know that we were a couple!"

This did not change the fact, however, that my husband was a quiet man who needed a bit of solitude every now and then. For that reason, every so often, I would leave Matthew at home for a couple hours in an evening just so that he could have some time to himself. Many times, this was after I had asked Matthew if he needed a little "me time." (That usually made him smile.) Then when I would kiss him goodbye, Matthew would stand at the door facing me. He would often take both of his hands and place them on my upper arms. Then he would look me fully in the eyes and say these exact words very slowly and deliberately, "*Be careful!* I would be *heartbroken* if anything happened to you."

One such time, I received a text from Matthew as I stood in the aisle of a store. I looked at my phone to read these words: "Where are you? I miss you."

My reply was "Really?"

Matthew responded, "Yes, when will you be home?"

Of course, I quickly wrapped things up at the store and headed to our apartment. When I arrived, the porch light was shining brightly for me, but all the other lights in the house had been turned off. Matthew loved candles every bit as much as I did. When I stepped inside, the whole apartment was aglow with soft candlelight. Only a brief minute later, Matthew walked slowly toward me, wrapped me in his arms, and welcomed me home with a gentle beautiful kiss.

One day, Matthew opened up a conversation with these words: "Do you know what I think makes us get along so well?"

I replied, "*Tell me.*"

He responded, "I really believe it's because we're both *givers*." He went on to explain that he had always been a giving type of person and therefore had carried that on into relationships with girls he had dated. Then he explained that sometimes the girl was more a *taker* than a giver. He said, "Eventually, the effort is so one-sided that the giver feels a real strain on the relationship." Continuing on, he said, "What I came to realize is that the *taker* is usually *happy* while the *giver* just becomes tired of feeling that they are being taken for granted." He added, "Becky, that's why we do so well together! You and I both give to each other in every part of this marriage. That's why we're both happy."

I remember being told something interesting by a mother of two little girls that I used to teach. She and her husband did not marry until they were in their thirties. This sweet lady had said to me, "One benefit of not marrying until later in life is that you don't take each other for granted." She added, "Maybe that's because you remember all too well what it feels like to be lonely." Well, I do personally know *that* to be an absolute fact, and so did Matthew.

Even with household chores, we didn't take each other for granted. We shared responsibilities. I would cook on the week*nights* and he would cook on the week*ends*. (Believe it or not, he asked if I would *mind* this arrangement!) Matthew loved to try new recipes. He was a *good* cook and an even *better* baker. Trust me, it was a real treat to have him make dinner! If Matthew decided that he was not in the mood to cook during the weekend, he would take me out to dinner.

We both knew how to do laundry, but I enjoyed doing it more than he did. I cannot tell you how many times he *thanked* me for doing his laundry for him. It was not unusual for Matthew to help me clean the house either. Matthew said that his mother had once told both he and his brother that they needed to be willing to share household duties with a wife one day if she also worked a full-time job. Another thing that often surprised me was that Matthew *always* helped me to put groceries away when we returned home from shopping. I had not expected any of this from a husband.

Speaking of grocery shopping, we would do one big shopping trip a month. As Matthew pulled his wallet from his pocket to pay the cashier on our first of these many trips, he happened to look down at me, noticing that my eyes were filling with tears. Minutes later, as he pushed the cart through the parking lot toward our vehicle, Matthew asked, "Why were you crying back there?"

I answered, "Never before in my life have I been able to buy everything that looked good to me. I could never have afforded to do that on my own, and I feel overwhelmingly blessed."

Matthew replied, "I'm glad that I've made your life better." He then added, "I *wanted* to do that for you." From that time on, Matthew would make a point to look at me as he paid for our groceries…until one day, literally months down the line, he saw no tears. That day, as we left the store, he leaned down and said, "I'm proud of you. You didn't cry this time."

Matthew and I did not take romance for granted either. Sometimes, I would write little notes and tuck them in with Matthew's lunch before he left for work or in his suitcase if he was leaving on a business trip. At first, I wondered if he would find this kind of silly. Instead, Matthew seemed to love it. I would sometimes see him check his lunch bag to see if there was a note inside. When I would see him reach inside the bag to pull out the note, I would say, "Hey! That's for later! You haven't even left the house yet!" Matthew also regularly left little notes for me around the house. One simply said, "Just wanted to remind you that I love you." Each of these treasured notes I have kept.

To celebrate each wedding anniversary, Matthew bought me a dozen red roses and took me on a short, little overnight getaway. He did all the planning, each time researching in advance to find a couple great places to eat, always including one elegant restaurant with candlelight. Also, after completing his research online, he would reserve a beautiful hotel room. He would also top off each of those hotel stays by ordering room service at some point. Not long ago, I read in one of Matthew's journal entries the following words written in his handwriting: "Becky, my wife, is a gift from God. I love her and I will cherish her." This explains why I never one day doubted the love of my husband.

## Chapter 20

I t is absolutely true that Matthew was extremely kind, tender, and loving. This husband of mine was no pushover, however! Matthew was too strong a man for that. My husband was a take-charge kind of guy. I honestly loved that! I had always known that I would not easily respect a man who did not have a stronger personality than I did. Matthew was exactly what I needed. He was my perfect match, my completer.

I personally believe that communication is the key to a good relationship of any sort. I have already mentioned that one of our best qualities as a couple was the fact that we communicated very well. To illustrate, I'll share a perfect example of that. Before marriage, Matthew had been told by many that I was usually late for everything. I was known for either being *right* on time or, more often than that, being a little late. I am certain that I did not know what it felt like to ever arrive *early* to anything.

I found out quickly in our dating relationship that Matthew *despised* being late. This difference between us could have been a constant source of controversy in a marriage…yet it wasn't. It was not an issue of contention because of a simple conversation that Matthew had with me shortly before we married. I have no idea how long he considered, or how hard he contemplated the words he chose to say to me, but I will admit that it was nothing short of brilliant!

One day, Matthew had said, "Becky, there is something we need to discuss before we get married. You know I've been told that you are usually late for everything. You also know that I *never* am. So I was thinking about how we could handle this. I am willing to compromise a little…if you will, as well. I normally like to arrive someplace half an hour or more early, but I can live with fifteen to twenty minutes early instead. I do realize that we have two cars. So I was thinking, if you cannot work on this time schedule, we can drive separately. That way, you can come when you're ready, and I will not be late." Matthew did not lecture, tease, or condemn. He simply stated the way it was going to be.

As I said already, his tactic was brilliant! After being single until I was forty-four years old and driving places by myself all the time, I was not about to be left behind! I finally had a husband to ride in the car with! Perhaps it is needless to say, but I'll say it anyway: never one time did Matthew have to leave me behind in almost two-and-a-half years of marriage. I knew my husband meant business, which meant that I had to change my ways if I wanted to ride with him.

There were at least a couple times that Matthew and I would be eating dinner at home when he would notice that I was being unusually quiet. When this happened, Matthew would ask me, "What's wrong?"

I would sometimes respond with the word, "Nothing."

His retort was "I can *tell* something is wrong. What is it? Is it *me*?"

My reply would be "I don't want to talk about it."

I can still picture the scene as Matthew would deliberately lay down his fork. (I need you to understand here that my husband loved his food!) I knew that this meant he was serious. Matthew would then lean across the table, look me directly in the eyes, and begin to speak matter-of-factly. He would say, "Well, neither of us is going to leave this table until we talk about it. I don't care if it *is* about me or if it isn't. If you don't tell me what's wrong, we can't fix the problem. What's up?"

I would finally tell him what was bothering me and we would sort the thing out. I *loved* the way he handled me.

Matthew did not shy away from confrontation as I did. Yet even though he did not mind being direct and straightforward with me, Matthew *did* make a deliberate attempt to be kind and genuinely considerate of my feelings. It is true, I had always known that

I needed a strong husband; but I guarantee that if Matthew had been mean-spirited or domineering, I can promise I would not have responded to him as I did. I thought about that recently. If I had married a man who yelled at me or talked down to me as though I were a child, I believe I would have done the same right back to him. There is no doubt God knew that even Matthew's temperament would blend perfectly with mine.

# Chapter 21

My Matthew was such a unique individual. His mother has referred to him as "an old soul." He had a genuine tenderness in his heart when it came to older folks and little children. As I've illustrated already, Matthew was gentle, compassionate, and very kind. In fact, his kindness was the first characteristic I used to describe him to those who hadn't met him yet.

After being married to Matthew for only a short time, he shared a story with me that proved that this gentle kindness was part of his inherent nature, from the time he was just a boy. One day, after I mentioned some facts I had just taught my fourth-grade students about the monarch butterfly, Matthew commented, "Did I ever tell you *my* story about a monarch?"

When I answered, "No, you didn't," he began to share. I was told that when he was in either first or second grade, Matthew had found an orange butterfly that had had one of its wings nearly torn in half and could no longer fly. He took the butterfly into his house, found some superglue, and carefully glued its wing back together. The butterfly was kept in a box in his bedroom, as I recall. Matthew would let it out for a few minutes each day to exercise its wings until he felt it had the strength to be set free. When the day had finally come for the creature's release, Matthew told me that he, as a young boy, had proudly walked out to his front porch, down a few steps, and onto the sidewalk. Here he bid farewell to his successfully repaired butterfly. After watching it happily flutter up into the air and across the street, to Matthew's chagrin, right before his very eyes, a bird swooped down and snatched the monarch in its beak. I gasped as Matthew told me the brutal end to this touching story! To me, it sounded like something that would only happen in an animated movie!

So yes, Matthew was my gentle giant! Matthew was also a man of physical and spiritual strength and a man who possessed impeccable character. Yet one of the personality traits that I enjoyed the most in my husband was his dry witty sense of humor. For instance, when Matthew and I had just started dating, we were sitting on bleachers, watching our first high school basketball game together at the school where I taught. Several minutes into the game, Matthew had turned to me and said, "Wow, I don't know how they do that!"

I asked, "Do what?"

Matthew answered, "Run full-court...over and over."

I lowered my eyebrows, looked at him, and said, "What are you talking about? You know that's how the game is played."

He turned his head, focusing his attention back to the boys on the court, and said, "The only way you could get *me* to do that is if someone hung a Twinkie from the hoop."

Now, this wasn't even remotely true because Matthew played high school *football* from ninth grade through the end of his senior year. He could have gone on to play in college, in fact, if he had accepted one of the scholarships that had been offered. He had only wanted to make me laugh.

I always knew that I needed someone who could do that—someone who could make me laugh. I've never enjoyed being around people who take themselves too seriously. In my classroom, in fact, one of my favorite teaching tools was humor. I completely love to watch a child laugh. I've always believed it is easier to learn when you are having fun. I am quite certain that Matthew and I made each other laugh nearly every day.

A good friend and fellow teacher of mine by the name of Lisa would walk with me for exercise several times a week while our students were in a particular class that neither of us taught. Of course, as we walked, we would talk. She would often ask me how things were going between Matthew and me. I never minded telling her either!

During one particular conversation, I mentioned again how much Matthew made me laugh and how fun it was to live with him. This time, she turned to look at me and said, "Becky, do you realize how unique that is in a marriage?"

I responded, "No. It only means that we're happy!"

She continued, "I don't think so. My husband and I have a great marriage. We are happy too, but we don't make each other laugh every day." She finished by saying, "That's something special that you two share."

After living together for just a short while, Matthew noticed how I love things to be neat and orderly. I never keep paperwork of any kind on my bedroom dresser. Because of this, Matthew thought it would be funny to throw a single candy wrapper or gum wrapper on my dresser every so often, just to see how long it would take me to notice it. He would also toss wrappers into my purse if it was open. (That was only done in my presence, however, because he loved to see how it would annoy me.) One time, my grown-up husband licked a gummy bear (his favorite candy) and stuck the wet thing to my dresser mirror. He was pretty proud of himself for *that*!

I mentioned already that both of us were "instigators." That was the word Matthew used when he first pointed out the fact to me. My favorite example of this was before we had married. We were engaged, and I had gone on a two-week vacation with my sister's family to the Outer Banks in North Carolina where Matthew would be joining us for the last few days. I knew for a fact that Matthew did not approve of tattoos, but I wanted to have a little fun and see what kind of reaction I would get if he thought I had gotten one. Just before he came down to join us, I had paid to have a henna tattoo of Matthew's name handwritten across my ankle. When he arrived, I couldn't wait to excitedly say, "Matthew! I have to show you what I've had done for you!" I then pointed out the name "Matthew" written neatly across my ankle.

Matthew dramatically hung his head and said in a voice heavy with disappointment, "Becky! You *know* what I think of tattoos!" I could not hold back my laughter any longer. Then I reassured him that it was only temporary and that I would be lucky if it stayed on for more than a week. I had far more fun with that incident than my poor fiancé did!

Without a doubt, it was fun to have two instigators living under the same roof! We had a tiny bathroom in our apartment. Matthew had a habit of hiking up his left leg and propping his foot up on the side of the bathtub as he brushed his teeth at the sink. Quite a number of times, I would walk in, stand right beside him, grab my own toothbrush, and hike my right leg up on a wooden box that held toiletry items. When I would begin to brush my teeth, alongside him, Matthew would look down at my leg propped up on the box and instantly realize that I was mocking him. He would then lower one eyebrow as he looked at my reflection in the mirror. One side of his mouth would curl upward though he tried his best not to smile.

Some days, I would pick up my toothbrush, only to find that the toothbrush was already wet. This would really irritate me. I would holler, "Matthew! Did you use my toothbrush?" The first time this happened, I thought he had grabbed the wrong one by accident; but I was mistaken. Each time this occurred, he would peek around the door of the bathroom with a big proud grin on his face. I would say, "That's gross, Matthew! Yours is right there. Why would you use mine?"

His response was always "I don't see the problem. We *kiss*!"

Once Matthew said to me, "I want you to know that a whole lot of what I say and do is just so that I can get a reaction out of you." He went on to say, "I love to hear what you'll say or see what you'll do."

# Chapter 22

Toward the very end of 2013, nearly two-and-a-half years into marriage, Matthew had planned a special date for the two of us. We would go to the restaurant where we had had our rehearsal dinner in 2011. This was not the first time that he and I had gone there on a date night since we married, but we were excited to see the restaurant decorated for Christmas. He and I would have dinner there on December 27, between Christmas and New Year's Day. With all the busyness of the holiday season, we had not had much quality time for just the two of us. This was a night we were much looking forward to.

I wish I did not feel the need to mention this…but I ruined that evening for the two of us. Matthew had done something that upset me, and I would not let it go. What could have been a beautiful evening together erupted into a horrible argument on the way home from the restaurant. After we had each spent much of the long ride home defending our cases, we endured the rest of the ride in silence. And to be honest, it was all over such a petty, insignificant thing. I tossed and turned in bed that night, unable to sleep. I was so upset with myself the longer I thought through the situation. If I had just been willing to overlook something, we could have had a wonderful evening together. Instead, it had been awful.

I got up out of bed after Matthew had fallen asleep and went to the computer to compose a letter of apology. It was lengthy but necessary. I printed it off, folded it, and taped the letter to the bathroom mirror so that Matthew would notice it first thing in the morning.

I began the letter by apologizing for my critical nature. I then took time to list many of the sweet things that Matthew did for me on a regular basis. I always made a point to thank him for these things as they happened, but now I needed him to know how much his consistent thoughtfulness meant to me. I also listed the qualities he possessed that made me so grateful to call him my husband. Of course, I again mentioned how sorry I was that all of that had been overlooked as I had made a mountain out of a molehill that evening. I closed the letter by reaffirming that I would love him until there was no more air to breathe.

Matthew forgave me and the issue was dropped. It was never brought up again. I still, nonetheless, felt that our argument that evening might have left an open wound in our marriage. It was the worst fight we had ever had. Approximately two weeks later, Matthew and I were sitting on our living room couch, having something to eat in front of the television. After we had finished, Matthew stood to take our dishes to the kitchen. As he did so, he began to hum. In the nearly two-and-a-half years of our marriage, I had only heard Matthew hum a few separate times. As he walked away, I simply said, "I *like* when you do that."

My husband turned to look at me; and with an amused look on his face, he asked, "Why?"

Looking directly into his dark brown eyes, I answered, "Because it makes me think you are happy."

Matthew stood rooted to the spot with both hands holding dishes. All amusement disappeared from his face as Matthew looked straight into my eyes and replied, "Oh, *I'm* happy. I'm *real* happy." Then he sweetly smiled and walked away. God knew how much I needed to hear that. All had been forgiven and we were okay again.

## Chapter 23

It was nearing the end of the first month of the year 2014. The weather was terrible. The snow did not seem to want to quit falling and the temperatures were frigid. Because the roads were so bad, school was being delayed on some days and canceled on others. Matthew's mom and grandma lived an hour away from us; and we had planned our monthly trip to visit them on Saturday, January 25. Because many inches of snow were expected to fall throughout that day, however, my mother-in-law called Matthew and told him that we should stay home.

On Sunday, the twenty-sixth of January, the roads were too dangerous to run the Sunday school bus routes for our church. In fact, Sunday school in general was canceled for all of us. We only had one morning service and Matthew was asked to open that service in prayer. Before the preaching began, our pastor announced that he was canceling the evening service also due to the hazardous road conditions and the fact that more snow was being forecasted. Since we now had an unexpected free evening ahead of us, I made a phone call on the way home to place an order for pizza that Matthew had been craving for much of that month. After picking up a pepperoni pizza from Pizza Hut, we stopped by a movie rental store and picked up two DVDs that we could watch that afternoon and evening.

Matthew had to work the next day, which was Monday, the twenty-seventh, but school went from a delay to a cancellation for me. Our high school basketball game that was scheduled for that night was called off as well.

On Tuesday morning, January 28, Matthew sent me a text message from his work to say that it was fifteen degrees below zero. He suggested that I go outside on my lunch break at school to start up my little red Volkswagen Beetle and let it run a bit due to the cold. On his way home at the end of the day, Matthew called me about four forty, as he always did while driving home from work. Then he opened our kitchen door about 5:00 p.m., as usual, as I was putting the finishing touches on dinner. Our tall pub-style table-for-two was set, with a candle burning in the center of it, which had been our tradition for the entirety of our short marriage.

Matthew had come home especially stressed about the workday that had just ended. I cannot recall the reason why exactly. This was Tuesday, however, and he always went to bagpipe lessons after dinner on Tuesday nights. That always relaxed him. My Matthew was a worrier, sometimes carrying much of the weight of the world on his shoulders…yet he never liked for *me* to worry. When we had finished eating, Matthew surprised me by announcing, "I'm not going to go to my pipe lessons tonight."

I asked, "Why not?"

A guilty smile turned up the corners of his mouth as Matthew replied, "I haven't practiced all week." Then he added, "I think I'll just hang with you tonight."

We discussed some ordinary husband-and-wife topics, such as bills that would be coming up. Matthew also told me that he felt we were nearly ready to make our first extra mortgage payment on the duplex we had bought six months before. (While the interest rates had been especially low, we were able to purchase the house that we had rented since marriage.) After that conversation had ended, I said, "Well, Matthew, if you are staying home with me, we have to do something to burn off some of that stress." I hesitantly asked, "Do you want to exercise?"

Secretly, I was hoping he would say no. Instead, he said, "All right." We had started at the beginning of January to work out, using an exercise DVD with Jillian Michaels from *The Biggest Loser*. We had already become rather hit-and-miss with it, however.

When Matthew and I had first begun working out together, Matthew would use his ten-pound hand weights and I would use my one-pound weights. His ten-pounders were heavier than necessary for the exercise routine, so we had looked in the pantry for canned goods to use instead. After that, Matthew would lift two cans of Dinty Moore beef stew. Well, we had recently been hungry for Dinty Moore! Of course, that meant that he had to find new hand weights for this evening. He chose two cans of pie filling, one apple and one blueberry.

There was one segment in the exercise routine where Matthew liked to watch me. I would always catch him smiling while we would squat with legs apart and twist our upper bodies from side to side while throwing punches into the air. I also got a kick out of watching him during that move because he would bounce a little as he twisted back and forth. On this one night, we decided to turn and face each other while throwing the punches. It made both of us laugh.

Our evening went from good to even better. I was so happy that Matthew had decided to stay home with me. I know that he was too. I remember looking at our alarm clock to see that the time was ten thirty that night, just before I fell asleep in Matthew's arms.

It is not unusual for me to get up several times throughout the night, but Matthew seldom ever did. On this particular night, however, he awoke as I came back into the bedroom somewhere around one thirty in the morning. As I climbed back into bed beside him, Matthew asked, "*What* are you *doing* over there?"

I laughed a little and said, "Nothing! I just came back from the bathroom."

He said, "You'd better watch it or I'll bounce you right out of bed!" I laughed. He got out of bed then also.

After returning to the room a few minutes later to lie back down beside me, I said, "Matthew, you had fallen asleep earlier without your mask. Would you put it on please?" (Matthew had sleep apnea and had to wear a sleep-mask with his CPAP machine.) He easily obliged and we both fell back to sleep.

My Matthew never opened his eyes on this earth again.

## Chapter 24

For a reason that none but God Himself can know and understand, my beloved husband was taken to heaven early that morning of January 29, 2014. At barely more than an hour after we had last spoken, I awoke, noticing that the sound under Matthew's mask had changed. I could no longer hear the sound of his breathing.

Every possible valiant effort to revive him was attempted—first, by myself being coached by the 911 operator, then by first responders, paramedics, and finally, emergency room staff.

One of the paramedics who had arrived at our home was responsible for keeping me away from our bedroom as they worked on Matthew. I made my way back into our room often enough, however, to know that two different men traded off performing CPR on him before the paddles were used to shock Matthew's heart. When the decision was made to transport my husband to the hospital, I was told that they would not let me ride in the back of the ambulance with Matthew. The paramedic that I previously mentioned explained that I would need to have my car at the hospital. That man spoke gently and patiently to me as he said, "Get your coat and put on some shoes." After I had done those things, he said, "Now find your car keys and your purse." He must have realized that I was not even able to think for myself during those moments when time seemed to stand still. The other paramedics had begun to transport Matthew to the waiting ambulance. When I had what I needed, this paramedic walked out with me to my car then climbed into the ambulance himself.

Once at the hospital, I was dragged away against my wishes from the "trauma 1" room in the emergency department of Butler Memorial Hospital. A member of the hospital staff ushered me into a special family conference room. My mom and dad, my sister Amy, my brother-in-law Aaron, and my pastor and his wife, Cara, would join me there. My mother-in-law was on her way to Butler, being driven that hour-long distance by Matthew's uncle Tony. My father-in-law was in St. Louis at the time.

Before my mother-in-law could arrive, the ER doctor came in to join the rest of us in that conference room. The doctor sat down very slowly. Then leaning forward to rest his forearms on his lap, he looked directly at me. I remember listening to the sentence I had previously heard only on television, as the doctor spoke these words: "Despite our best efforts, we were not able to revive your husband."

I remember stating, "I don't want to *BE* here anymore!" Somehow I was able to focus enough to ask if they had ever been able to find a heartbeat or a pulse. I was told that they had not. For this reason, although my husband's time of death was pronounced at three forty-six early that Wednesday morning, I believe with all my heart that Matthew's soul entered heaven as he lay sleeping beside me approximately one hour sooner on that darkest day of my life, January 29, 2014.

When the doctor left that little conference room, I knew that I had to call Matthew's mom. The others also went out into the hall to make phone calls. I only remember Amy remaining beside me as I placed the call to Matthew's mother. I still recall holding the phone away from my ear as my mother-in-law cried and cried. After making that gut-wrenching phone call, my head began to jerk back and forth uncontrollably. I reached up, trying to hold my head steady with my hands, as my sister softly said, "It will stop. You're just going into shock." This would happen three more times before I left the hospital.

Matthew was a young, strong, seemingly healthy and vibrant thirty-seven-year-old man. An autopsy would be performed, which would show that he did *not* have a heart *attack*. It was explained that Matthew's heart had simply stopped beating.

In that quiet early hour of the morning, it seemed to me that every hope and dream of happiness had been torn out of my life. I was utterly *broken*.

My biggest struggle in life, however, had only just begun.

I can recall a conversation that Matthew and I had had one day, several months before. We had been seated side by side on our living room couch, talking about what we thought heaven would be like. Both of us were aware that the Bible speaks of heavenly mansions for us to live in. I remember looking into Matthew's eyes that day and saying, "I sure hope God lets us share a mansion together!"

Matthew's witty response was "Well, if He doesn't, I think it will work out just fine for you to come visit mine between two and three o'clock every day."

I said, "Oh, that's very generous of you! You would let me see you for one hour a day?"

He had laughed.

I also had said to him during that conversation, "Well, I sure am glad that I married someone nine years younger! At least I'm pretty confident that I'll die first." Then I added with much feeling, "I don't *ever* want to live without you again!"

Matthew's soft-spoken reply was "Becky, you don't know that you'll die first. No one can know that."

My response was, "No, but I think it's a fairly safe bet!"

Matthew then had found a way to turn the conversation to more lighthearted things. (He never liked to see me sad.) I watched as a smart-alecky look spread across his handsome face. Then Matthew had said, "Well, if you *do* die first, I *so* know what I'll have you laid out in!"

Very curious, I had cocked my head to the side and asked, "Oh, you *do*? Do you?"

An ornery smile stretched from one side of his mouth to the other as he answered, "I will have you dressed in denim!"

I raised one eyebrow and replied, "If you have me laid out in denim, I will *so* find a way to come back and haunt you!"

Matthew threw his head back and laughed loudly. (He knew very well that, as a rule, I prefer to dress "up" rather than dress "down.")

To be truly and completely honest, when I spoke the words "till death do us part" in my wedding vows, I never even *considered* that I might have to face Matthew's untimely death. After all, I had waited for most of my life to *meet* my "dream come true." I falsely assumed that I would be allowed to grow old with him.

# Chapter 25

We all were permitted to go in to the trauma room together to say our goodbyes to Matthew. After my mother-in-law and Matthew's uncle Tony had left the hospital, my family and the hospital staff were kind enough to let me have time alone with Matthew's sleeping form. When it appeared as though I might never leave him, however, Amy and Aaron joined me again in the trauma room. I am certain it had to be uncomfortable for them as they watched me stroking Matthew's hair, tracing my fingers over his face, and caressing his hand as I held it in mine. I couldn't seem to stop myself from touching him.

Then my brother-in-law gently said, "Becky, Matthew wouldn't want you to still be here. He wouldn't want you to see him like this."

After I agreed to leave, they walked with me out into the hallway. As I turned back to take one final look, I glanced at a clock on the wall above where Matthew lay. The time was 6:00 a.m. I could hardly believe I had been permitted to stay so long. As the metal doors swung shut behind me, my head began to jerk back and forth in shock again for the fourth and final time.

Upon leaving the hospital that morning, my mind was completely and absolutely numb. My life, as I knew it, had ended. I had no idea what to do from this point on, nor did I have any ounce of desire to continue living without Matthew. I was so upset that I had been left here when my husband had been taken. My goodness! He and I were together so much of the time! I could not understand why God had not chosen to take us *together* in an accident, if He needed

Matthew that badly. God could have easily arranged for our car to hit a tree. Snow was everywhere. There were plenty of slick roads. None of this made any sense!

I did not know what I possibly could have done to deserve Matthew being removed from my life. I even wondered if God took my husband because I loved him *too* much. But then, I quickly recalled listening to a sermon by a radio preacher, as I was driving home from work roughly a year before. After hearing that sermon in my car, I came to the realization that I had placed Matthew on a pedestal that he was never meant to be placed on. Before arriving home that day, I had asked the Lord's forgiveness for coming to a place where I felt that I needed my husband in my life *every bit as much* as I needed the God who had brought my husband *to me*. I had gotten my priorities out of kilter. I went straight home and told Matthew about it that day. When I told him about my talk with God, and about asking God for forgiveness, Matthew quietly said, "I wondered. And I'm glad you made things right." For this reason, I cannot believe that Matthew was taken as a punishment to me.

I am certain that one of my family members drove me home from the hospital in my car that morning of January 29. I remember that they would not allow me to drive myself anywhere for a while. I know that I was told to try to sleep when I got home. I did lie down in bed; but as you can imagine, sleep did not come. Instead, my phone started ringing, almost as soon as I laid my head on the pillow. After answering the first call, requesting Matthew's organs, I could not bring myself to answer the phone or to reply to a text message again that day. While it was yet early in the morning, I heard a knock on my door and answered it to see a first responder. He had been sent to retrieve a medical bag that one of the other men had left behind. That was likely as difficult for the first responder as it was for me.

Much of that Wednesday remains a blur. I know I was supposed to make a call to the funeral home to make arrangements, but I could not do it. In a short while, my sister Amy had come to my house. She made the call for me. I was told to go down to the funeral home to pick up some necessary forms to fill out. Again, I could not bring myself to do it. Amy went for me. While Amy was doing what she could, my mom was making calls from her home to the cemetery, where years before, she and my dad had made arrangements to be buried. As my parents were "prearranging," they had chosen to purchase a third burial plot for my use in case I never married. This plot, I would now be able to use for both Matthew and I. His casket would be buried twice as deep, leaving room for my casket to be laid above his one day.

So much had to be done, but I simply moved around as in a daze. The only thing that mattered to me greatly was that no one moved any of Matthew's things. His slippers were on the floor beside his brown La-Z-Boy recliner and a set of clothes that he had planned to wear to work that morning was lying in a neat pile on the arm of another chair in our living room. Matthew would often set his clothes there the night before so that he wouldn't need to wake me when he first got up at five fifteen in the morning. Caring, thoughtful people began coming to my door bringing food for me and for my family members who would surely be arriving. Everything felt surreal, yet I knew this was actually happening. Life was moving on even though it felt completely wrong that it should.

Amy drove me to the funeral home the next day to make arrangements for Matthew. My parents, Matthew's parents, and my sister were there to help me think through and plan what needed to be done. While we were all seated around a large rectangular conference table, going over some final details involving the funeral, the funeral director looked at me and asked, "Do you want to speak at the funeral?"

I had never contemplated that question. In a voice that displayed all the shock I felt inside, I asked, "Do I *have* to?"

He kindly laid his hand on my arm and said, "No, of course, you don't. I just needed to ask."

As Amy drove me home following that meeting, she drove down the lengthy Main Street in my hometown of Butler, Pennsylvania. At one point, I said to her, "Look at all these people walking and laughing and going about their merry ways as if it's any other day! Their lives are going on as usual and mine feels like it has ended!"

After arriving home, it didn't take long for me to realize that I *did* have to speak at Matthew's funeral. God tenderly reminded me that Matthew and I had begun praying since the beginning of January that God would present us opportunities that year to be a witness to family and friends of God's love and goodness. We also wanted to share with them the fact that God could be *their* personal Savior as we had asked Him to be *ours*. I knew that this was an *opportunity* unlike any I would ever be given again in this life. *Together*, we had asked God to let us be a witness for Him. Matthew's death had provided the opportunity. The very least I could do was to speak.

## Chapter 26

I had never been a *needy* person in all of my adult life until now. That first night without Matthew, however, I could not bear the thought of being left alone. I asked if either my sister or my mom would stay with me overnight. My other sister Colleen was flying in from Tennessee. My brother-in-law Larry would be driving up, bringing my nephew and niece with him. Colleen and Larry would stay at my house until after the funeral.

Every night for a week or two, either my mom or one of my sisters would sleep next to me in bed. My heart still hurts when I realize how hard this had to be for them. I was asking them to sleep where Matthew had taken his final breath. Night after night, the one who stayed with me would be awakened at some point by my uncontrollable sobbing. Each of them would take their turn trying to console me until I would eventually cry myself to sleep again in utter exhaustion. For another several days after my mom and sisters had returned to their homes, a dear friend and fellow teacher of mine, Karen, would come and sleep on my couch at night. Karen was also our upstairs tenant at the time and offered to stay downstairs over-night with me until I was ready to be left alone. (If that isn't a true friend, I don't know what is.)

Strangely enough, not one time did I ever feel uncomfortable about sleeping in the bed that Matthew and I had shared. This has always amazed me. Oddly, it continues to bring me comfort to sleep where Matthew had last slept beside me. To this day, I will sometimes hug his pillow to me as I fall asleep.

I could not bring myself in those first initial days after losing Matthew to *speak to God*. It sounds conflicting when I say that I was willing to speak at Matthew's funeral, feeling strongly that this was what God wanted me to do. Yet I could not speak directly *to God*. I could not find any words to say to Him! I could not feel God's presence with me either. This was a very foreign and frightening feeling to me. I know that in His Word, God promises never to leave us or forsake us. But yet, it felt very much like He *had* forsaken me. Since I couldn't have Matthew's arms around me again in this life, I wanted, at least, to feel that God's arms were holding me in a comforting embrace…yet I could not. Those first days of grieving were the very loneliest and darkest days of my entire existence.

Not only did I find it impossible to speak to God at this time. I could not bring myself to read my Bible either. My family knew that the Scriptures would be a comfort to me. For this reason, either my mom or one of my sisters (whoever had been the one to stay overnight with me) would read portions of God's Word to me the next morning. Afterward, they would ask if I would like to pray. When I would explain that I just *couldn't*, they did not condemn or lecture. They would simply pray out loud *for me*.

Matthew's viewing was set for Sunday, February 2, from one to four and seven to nine at the funeral home. The funeral itself would take place at our very own Calvary Baptist Church on Monday morning, February 3. I remember thinking that it was unfortunate for Matthew's viewing to fall on Super Bowl Sunday, but I had no need to be concerned. An astonishingly large amount of people made their way to Butler, Pennsylvania, to pay their respects to my husband that Super Bowl Sunday. I am confident that Matthew never had any idea just how many lives he touched in his thirty-seven years on earth. At one point, the funeral director came up to me and to my mother-in-law to tell us that people were lined up down the street that cold, winter day, waiting to come inside. He added that some of them had graciously waited for two to two-and-a-half hours to talk to us. It was necessary to extend the visiting hours to five o'clock. We came back again at 7:00 p.m. My in-laws and I were overwhelmingly touched by the many people who traveled from near and far to be there for us that day. Such beautiful kind words were spoken on behalf of our Matthew.

My pastor had told me that if I still wanted to speak at Matthew's funeral, it would be a good idea to type out what I wanted to say and to print the words in a large font so that I would be able to read it through my tears. He also told me that if I couldn't get through it, I could hand the paper off to him and he would finish reading for me. God helped me to read every word that I wanted to say; and for that, I will always be grateful. I felt so strongly that I needed to speak in honor of my husband and our Lord. And I believed that Matthew was going to be listening the whole time. To me, it felt like this was the last gift I could give him.

Nearly two-and-a-half years before, Matthew and I had been married in the same church where his funeral would be held. On the day of our *wedding*, the church auditorium was nearly filled to capacity. As mentioned before, we had a large wedding, with approximately three hundred guests. It is possible, though, that the auditorium was every *bit* as full on that Monday of Matthew's funeral. One large section was filled with Matthew's coworkers, fellow supervisors, and his superiors from US Steel. I was told that some divisions of US Steel had shut down for the day so that they could attend my husband's funeral.

I had asked Matthew's bagpipe instructor, Mr. Larry Morrison, if he would play "Amazing Grace" on the bagpipes at the funeral. This kind and talented man did a chillingly beautiful job and refused to let me pay for his services, saying that Matthew was his *friend*. Both Matthew's dad and Matthew's longtime best friend, Jeff Halliday, also spoke during the funeral service. The day was a lovely touching tribute to my husband's beautiful life.

# Chapter 27

Across our country, Valentine's Day would be celebrated only eleven days after Matthew's funeral. Matthew and I had shared Valentine's Day twice together as husband and wife. I remember Matthew saying to me, "It's so great to finally have a wife of my own on Valentine's Day!" We had celebrated that date both years with a special dinner, cards, and gifts, of course; but we had never done anything out of the ordinary. Well, this year of 2014, Matthew had decided that we should do the day up *big*.

Matthew had already booked a room in a particular Marriott Hotel that I had always wanted to stay in. Many times, I would comment on how pretty that hotel was as we passed it heading to and from Matthew's mom's house. When I would ask if we could stay there sometime, Matthew would tell me that it was kind of silly to rent a room only forty minutes away from home. Wouldn't you know, though, he had reserved us a room there for this upcoming Valentine's Day. After surprising me with that news, he had announced where he would take me for dinner that evening before we arrived at the hotel. Then Matthew surprised me once again by stating that he had made reservations for the two of us to have massages at a spa down the road from the Marriott for the next afternoon. I was so excited!

Now that Matthew was gone, my brother-in-law Aaron graciously volunteered to call the hotel and the spa to cancel our reservations, explaining that Matthew had died suddenly. I remain thankful to Aaron for making those cancellations so that I did not have to.

Valentine's Day continues to be one of the most difficult of holidays for me.

As I have already explained, I found it almost impossible to feel God's presence during the first couple weeks after losing my husband. I *was* now able to speak to God in prayer again, however. I also placed my own Bible on a shelf and began reading Matthew's instead. This was one of the most precious decisions I ever made. I take Matthew's Bible to church with me and use another of his Bibles for my personal devotions, to this day. I plan to continue this practice for the rest of my life. I cannot explain how it touches my heart to read the notes that Matthew has written all through his Bibles. Hundreds of times, I have noticed that he has underlined or highlighted the same verses that I had also marked in my own Bible. I love knowing that God had been speaking through His Word to my husband in the same way that He had been speaking through His Word to me.

Something happened to me on that dreaded Valentine's Day of 2014 that I hope I will never forget. I had needed to get a long list of items from Walmart. I had been avoiding going out in public, as much as I possibly could, however, because I was regularly dissolving into tears. Amy offered to go with me to make it easier. When the shopping was completed, I remember pushing my empty shopping cart toward the cart-return area after we had finished loading all the bags into my car. After the shopping cart had been emptied, the only thing remaining in it was my new purse. This beautiful Coach purse had been given to me for Christmas by Matthew—my last gift from him. I specifically recall the top zipper being wide open and a $100 gift card from Matthew's brother and sister-in-law lying on top, in full view.

It was a sunny Valentine's Day afternoon and the parking lot was full of cars. As I pushed my cart into the cart-return, my phone rang, and I answered it. After leaving my cart where it belonged, I distractedly turned, with only my phone in hand, to walk back toward my sister, who was waiting in the car.

It was not until I arrived home and had brought all the bags into my kitchen when I realized that I could not find my purse. I was beside myself! All my personal information, credit cards, gift cards, a wallet full of money—*everything* was inside that last Christmas gift that Matthew would ever give me! Amy looked up the phone number for Walmart so I could call them. Of course, I realized it was almost pointless to ask if a brand-new Coach purse had been turned in, especially one that had been left in an empty buggy in broad daylight. I could not even hold myself together enough to speak intelligently into the phone. Because I was crying so much, Amy took the phone out of my hand and explained to the kind lady on the other end of the line just what had happened. There was a pause, and I heard Amy say, "Really? Yes, I'll bring her back to the store." Amy ended the call and said with emphasis, "Becky, someone turned your purse in!" She knew, as well as I did, how unlikely that was to happen. She added, "You have to go into the store yourself to claim it so they can identify you by your driver's license."

When the purse was handed over to me, I asked through eyes brimming with tears, "Did the person who turned it in leave their name and number so I could thank them?" When I was told they had not, I asked if it was a little old lady who brought my purse inside. *This* lady smiled and said, "No! It was a young man, probably in his twenties!" By the way, every single item was still in that purse! Not *one* thing was missing. It remains difficult, still today, for me to put into words how overwhelmed my heart was at that moment with one particular fact. God knew that I could not *feel* His presence. He, therefore, created a situation in which I would be forced to *see* that He was still watching over me and taking care of my needs when no one but God could have made that situation right. I still like to imagine Matthew watching this young man from heaven when my purse was first noticed. I imagine Matthew whispering, "C'mon, Buddy, do the right thing! That purse belongs to my wife and she can't handle any more heartache right now. Take it inside! That's right! Atta boy! I knew you could do it." I may not have been able to *feel* God's presence, but I now knew beyond the shadow of a doubt that He was there!

And I don't believe it was any coincidence whatsoever that this proof of God's continuing love for me was shown on Valentine's Day.

# Chapter 28

I hardly recognized the person I had become in those first days of my journey through grief. The thought of trying to take things "one day at a time," as we so often hear, was too overwhelming for me. At this point, I could only concentrate on taking one "breath" at a time. I could not focus. I could not make decisions. I was extremely insecure. I recall the first time I was asked to write my signature on an important paper. I had signed my given name "Rebecca." Then without any hesitation, I began to write my maiden name "Walker" instead of "Yount." I became so angry with myself that I cried. Of course, it is true that I lost my husband, but my brain was trying to tell me that I had no more right to carry Matthew's last name. I cannot begin to count the many times this same situation arose. Again and again (exactly the way it had been when I first married), I would have to consciously think through which last name to write.

It took me some time to process, to comprehend that I did not instantly revert back to being *single* after the loss of my husband (regardless of how I am required to file taxes once again on my income tax return!) Although I had only been married for less than two-and-a-half years, the fact remained that I once *did* have a husband and I *had* indeed been his wife. Without any choice of my own, I found myself placed into a segment of society which has likely never been desired by *anyone*. I was now a widow. This was the one category in which I belonged. Being a widow, however, felt *nothing* like being single other than the fact that I was alone again. I have never before experienced pain like this. Honestly, I could not have imagined that *anything* could hurt this badly. I had lost the one who shared my dreams for all my tomorrows.

I was able to continue teaching the second semester of the 2013–2014 school year on autopilot. I only had two little fourth-grade students, my smallest class in twenty-three years of teaching. One student was my own niece Allison, and the other, her best friend in life, Victoria. (God knew that I needed a tiny naturally intelligent class this particular year.) It seemed as if those precious girls had formed an unspoken arrangement after I returned to the classroom, a week after Matthew had died. Every time they saw my eyes well up in tears, they would push their chairs back, stand up from their desks, and come up to put their little arms around me, one girl on one side and one on the other. They did not speak a word. They just felt that I needed a hug, and they knew they could do that. *God* knew I needed the hugs, and He knew I needed the compassion of those little girls.

I was not dealing well with the loss of my husband. All I wanted to do was sleep because I could almost make life go away when I slept. I even took every opportunity I could find at school to sleep. When the girls would go to recess, I would shut my classroom door and turn off the lights for those few short minutes. Then I would set the alarm on my phone and lay my head down on my desk to sleep until the alarm went off. At that time, I would turn the lights back on and open the door so my students would never realize I had been napping. During the classes that I did *not* teach, such as Bible class or gym class, I would nap on a couch in the school library or in my friend Jodie's kindergarten room, which was not in use during those times.

The hardest part of the days for me now were the mornings. Mornings were *horrible*! Upon waking, my first conscious thought was the realization that my husband was gone from this earth forever, and *that* realization knocked the breath out of me within the first waking moments of every day. Then I would sob until my heart felt it would break. I can honestly say that I know the following fact firsthand. Our *physical* heart can truly hurt when our *emotional* heart cannot bear the pain it holds. Even my physical heart ached constantly.

Amy and Aaron had thought of something that would help. They knew that I had been asking Matthew if we could get a dog like theirs. I was trying to get my husband to warm up to the idea of us having one of our own. Well, many members of my family, and some friends as well (even my former pastor and his wife), decided to contribute money and buy me a puppy that I would be allowed to choose from a breeder. They felt it would be a perfect *distraction*—a distraction that I needed to give me reason to get up in the mornings and a reason to think about a living creature in my home other than myself. They were right! My little "Sophie" is a fluffy white Coton de Tulear (related to the Maltese and the Bichon). She is hypoallergenic since I am allergic to most dogs; and she weighs all of thirteen pounds, now that she's fully grown. She is such a good little dog. I really *enjoy* her, and I'm not quite sure what I would do without her company.

After bringing Sophie home, I needed to house-train her, of course. My sister had already thought this through and met me every weekday morning in the school parking lot. She would drop my nephew Reed and my niece Allison off at school and trade them for my Sophie, who she would care for during the day. At the end of the day, Amy would bring Sophie back to the school when she returned to pick up Reed and Allie.

Amy also would pray with me inside her car each morning before she left the parking lot to head toward home. She would ask God to please heal my broken heart and to help me find purpose again in life. After praying with me like this for a while, but becoming more and more concerned about my well-being, she recommended that I ask my pastor and his wife to also pray with me in the pastor's office before school would begin. This, Pastor Ward and Cara faithfully did with me for many weeks.

I was amazed at how many little things bothered me greatly for a while. For instance, one of my fellow teachers had come into the school office one day, as I was making copies, or some such thing. She made a simple phone call to set up an appointment for a tanning session. As I listened, I became more and more agitated until I felt like I was going to come unglued. To me, this was nothing but petty and insignificant. Life was so much bigger than a tanning appointment! Now that I have healed enough to think logically again, I believe that what bothered me more than anything else was the fact that most of the lives around me had not changed to any large degree at all. *Mine* had.

My life had been turned upside down. *Everything* had changed for me, even my eating habits. I did not want to go home after school because that was when I would begin to prepare dinner for Matthew. I did not want to look at my kitchen clock when it was anywhere near 4:40 p.m. because that was the time Matthew would always give me a quick call on his way home from work. At 5:00 p.m., I could still picture him opening our kitchen door at the end of his workday.

I couldn't bear the thought of *cooking* in my kitchen now. When I would open any given cabinet, I could expect the tears to fall. The majority of the items inside those kitchen cabinets had belonged to Matthew. As a single man, he had taken great pleasure in collecting almost anything you would ever desire to use for cooking and baking. After we were married, we had often worked together on recipes while he taught me some of what he knew.

It would take fifteen months before I was willing to have anyone over to my home for dinner. (Matthew and I had had company in *several* times). That meal I finally served was a Mother's Day dinner for my mom, my mother-in-law, and Matthew's grandma. It wasn't until the two-year-and-two-month mark before I succeeded in making *myself* a full home-cooked dinner, like I used to make for Matthew. And in doing so, I had a full-fledged meltdown. On that day, I decided no longer to sit down to eat alone at our kitchen table. I now eat in front of the television so that I do not feel the weight of silence as much. Within seven months after losing Matthew, I had lost twenty-seven pounds through no attempt whatsoever.

An additional large burden lay heavily on my heart through the end of winter and into the spring of 2014. I was well aware that a potentially life-altering decision loomed ahead of me. Before the end of the school year, I was going to have to make a choice between continuing in the career that I loved (with the people I loved) or changing my place of employment.

It was necessary for me to earn a significantly larger income if I was going to keep the home that Matthew and I had purchased. We had been able to buy the house that we had been renting throughout our marriage—only six months before Matthew had passed away. This house had been divided years before into two completely separated apartments. We lived in the downstairs and benefited from the rental income of the upstairs apartment. Although we had purchased the house for an unbelievably good price, still we had to take out a thirty-year mortgage for it.

Matthew had taken good care of me by leaving me his life insurance. I had chosen to invest most of this, however, for my future since I was only forty-six years old when I lost Matthew. I did not (and still do not) believe it would have been as wise for me to use much of that money to pay off our house. Instead, I used it to pay off our car loan and his final expenses. Then I was helped to find a great financial adviser, who guided me in wisely investing the rest of Matthew's life insurance money. Matthew never expected to die at the age of thirty-seven, yet he provided for me in case he was not here to do it himself. Again, how blessed I was to have had a husband who loved me that much!

# Chapter 29

As mentioned already, I found my life now to be strangely unfamiliar. I also learned that my reactions were completely unpredictable after Matthew passed away. I could never guess how I was going to react to things. I found that so many ordinary occurrences of life had become terribly painful now.

Surprisingly, one of the most difficult things in my new life as a widow was to walk down an aisle of greeting cards. Matthew and I both took pride in choosing beautiful meaningful cards for each other. I noticed that both of us always chose cards with the words "husband" or "wife" printed on them. Maybe that was because I had waited so long to *have* a husband and he had waited so long to have a wife. It saddens me to think that I have no business even looking at those cards any longer.

I do, however, still have each note, letter, and card that Matthew ever wrote to me! I even saved one envelope on which he had written the two simple words, "My Becky," as he had done ever since we married. I treasured those notes and letters *then*, but they are priceless to me *now*. Matthew knew that *I* saved every little note that he wrote to me. But it wasn't until the anniversary of his second birthday spent in heaven that I found something hidden inside the back cover of two of his journals.

Matthew had a total of twelve journals in which he had been writing since he first began his walk with the Lord. After Matthew's death, I had started to read his journals. At first, I had not realized, though, that what appeared to be the inside back cover of each leather-bound book was actually a large concealed pocket. When I first reached inside one of those pockets, I pulled out a big handful of little notes that I had written to Matthew, including the notes that I would sometimes send in the lunch bags he would take for work. Of course, I grabbed another journal and found another handful of notes I had written to him, all neatly pressed flat. As you can imagine, the discovery of these hidden treasures caused a torrent of tears to cascade down my cheeks. That husband of mine had never given me the slightest hint whatsoever that he had saved any of the notes I had written him. I also found cards and letters galore in his dresser drawers. There is now not one letter or card that I recall giving to Matthew which I have not found since he has passed. My sweet husband was more sentimental than I ever realized!

It was *awfully* hard after Matthew's passing to hear so many well-meaning people say to me, "I know what you're going through." They would sometimes go on to tell me that they had lost a parent, a grandparent, an aunt, uncle, or a good friend. I know that these people meant well, and I understand that *every* loss hurts; but those losses are *not* the same as losing a beloved spouse. I was much more inclined to listen when a widow or widower tried to console me. I truly welcomed what they had to say…because *they* had been in my shoes (or at least in similar ones). To be perfectly truthful, the comment that meant the *most* to me was "I can't imagine what you're going through, but I love you and I'll be praying for you." *That* was *perfect*!

It didn't help at all when folks would say, "Remember that God works all things together for our good." Certainly, I knew that already; but I hurt so badly that it felt like they were rubbing sandpaper across a fresh wound. I found that the best thing people could do for me was to *listen*—just to listen to me talk about Matthew (even when I repeated the same stories over and over). I *loved* to hear anyone talk about him by name. I *still* do! I guess hearing Matthew's name acknowledges the fact that he was once here and that his life made a difference.

Especially when I had first lost Matthew, most people seemed to feel uncomfortable talking to me about him or even mentioning his name. I am sure they were concerned that it would only make me sad if they were to bring him up in conversation. Ironically, though, hearing other people's memories of Matthew warm my heart to this day and help me heal a little more—every time. After reading many books on grief and speaking to other widows, I find that this is common to *most* of us. We *love* to hear our departed spouse mentioned by name.

Actually, three young ladies were *invaluable* to me when it came to this issue. All three of these young women had been my students in both third grade and fourth grade. Each had drawn much closer to me as teenagers, and all of them had become precious friends of mine by the time they reached adulthood. Throughout the time that Matthew was in my life, and during the hardest years of my loss, these ladies—Tawnie, Stephanie, and Tianna—had faithfully attended the same church that I remain a member of. Each one of them had married and had begun their families before Matthew and I had even met. These girls knew me through and through. After I lost Matthew, they seemed to sympathize more easily, I think, simply because they and their husbands had only been married a few years longer than Matthew and I had. They knew I needed to talk and they were willing to listen. They would individually seek me out multiple times and tell me their own stories of what they loved and remembered about Matthew. I don't know what I would have done without their involvement in my life during this time when I was struggling so badly.

*Chapter 30*

One month and a half after Matthew had passed away, my dad was hospitalized with a blood infection that had taken away his ability to walk. While Matthew was still with us, my dad had had knee replacement surgery and had fought through the pain, recovering like a champ. And now he couldn't walk! After a weeklong stay in the hospital, Dad was admitted to the rehabilitation unit of a large local nursing home. This nursing home was only five minutes away from *my* home, so I would stop after school on most days to visit him. I was even allowed to bring my puppy, Sophie, with me. I believe it was good for Dad; but I *know* it was good for *me* to have some*one* else and some*thing* else to think about other than myself and my own loss. It was good for me to try to be an encouragement to my dad instead of going home to an empty house to cry.

Slowly, but surely, my seventy-nine-year-old dad worked and worked to regain the use of his legs. After one month and ten days, Dad was released to go home! I have always admired my dad for his consistently positive outlook on life and his amazing determination to fight through "the tough stuff." Once again, he had done that.

Dad got to be home for three days…but only three days. On that third day, I had gone to my parents' home to see how Dad was coming along. My mother had told me that he was losing strength again. I found my dad lying in bed, in the middle of that sunny day, looking horribly weak and discouraged. My mom had not been able to lift him and he had no strength to lift himself. I recall Mom standing by the bed, informing me that she was going to have to call the ambulance to take him to the hospital.

As I write this, I can vividly remember standing at the foot of my parents' bed as a dark ominous feeling came over me. It was as though a sheer-black curtain was slowly descending over my head. I had never seen my father look like this. Dad did not argue that he wanted to stay home. He did not look at me and say, "It's okay. I'm going to be all right." Those are the things I expected him to do—the things I expected him to say. But, as I recall, he said *nothing*. I could see from the look in his eyes that he knew he had no choice but to go.

I felt something change inside me during those brief moments of time. It was as though a light switch had been flipped. I had always heard that God will not give His children more than they can bear. But all of a sudden, for the first time in my life, I believed that God had lied. Wasn't it enough that I had had the love of my life so suddenly ripped away from me just three months before? Now it looked as though God was going to take away my father as well! In my opinion, this *was* more than I could bear!

By allowing myself to believe that God was being unfair to me, I caused myself to sink quickly into deep depression. I was being pulled into a dark pit of despair and I knew it. This was no longer ordinary, heart-wrenching grief. I had given ear to Satan or to one of his demons, whose wicked voice had led me to believe that God had forsaken this child of His, deliberately causing me more pain than I could possibly bear. I was done believing that God cared for me.

For two or three horribly dark days, I allowed Satan to have victory over my heart. I had given up on God, my Creator.

Yet in spite of this, God's merciful grace and His unfailing love found their way into my heart and into my conscious thought. While alone in my bedroom, everything suddenly became clear to me. There in the midst of my darkness, I was able to realize in my heart of hearts that I could not let Satan ruin my testimony, as he desired to.

For all of my adult years, I had endeavored to live my life in a way that would bring honor and glory to my Savior. On August 12 of 2011, the beautiful day that Matthew and I were happily joined together as husband and wife, Satan *had* to have felt defeat. Although

Matthew and I were marrying for the first time (later in life than most), we had NOT *settled* and we had *succeeded* in conducting our dating relationship honorably. God received glory from that, and nearly three hundred people were witness to the fact. On our wedding day, down to the last detail, our Lord was intentionally given much-deserved honor and praise for joining Matthew's life and mine together. Throughout our short years together as husband and wife, God had rewarded us with the blessing of an exceptionally happy marriage. This fact, in itself, had to aggravate Satan because our union was proof of what God could do with two lives sincerely seeking to please their Savior.

Very clearly, Satan intended now to convince me to join the ranks of other Christians who have turned their backs on God. As I came to the realization that Satan was doing his best to stamp out any honor I had ever succeeded in giving my Lord, I was *angry*... but I had absolutely no strength left to fight. I felt a very real warfare going on inside me...a more tangible spiritual battle than I had ever experienced in my life.

Finally, I knelt down beside my bed and begged forgiveness from the God of heaven. I told the Lord that I *knew* better than to doubt His love for me. He had loved me enough to send His only Son to die on a cross for me. He had given me countless blessings throughout my life. He had proven His love time and time again by answering specific prayers, just for me. He had brought *Matthew* into my life, when humanly speaking, our paths never should have crossed! God had *always* taken care of me. He was *not done* taking care of me now! God had a plan and He had reasons for doing what He was doing. God did not *expect* me to agree with Him or even to understand. He only wanted me to *trust* Him.

I know that many Christians had been praying for me. And even though no one on earth was aware of the particular spiritual warfare that I was battling for those two or three days, God answered the prayers that were prayed for me. I regret to admit that the devil absolutely did knock my feet out from under me. But God gently reached down to take hold of my weary hands and helped me to stand back up.

# Chapter 31

About three months before the end of the school year, I had asked my sister and brother-in-law to go with me to meet with my pastor (who was also our school administrator) and his wife, Cara, concerning my finances and my future at the school. I had shared all of my personal financial information already with Amy and Aaron. I had done the same, in fact, with my sister Colleen and her husband, Larry, while they stayed with me during the week of Matthew's funeral. My brother-in-law Larry may never realize just how grateful I will always be for the time he spent talking over these matters with me. I desired my family's input because I realized that I was not currently able to think clearly and logically on my own. As mentioned previously, it was very hard for me to *focus* or to make even *simple* decisions for a very long time after losing Matthew. I wanted Cara's input also. She was not only my pastor's wife. She has been a true friend of mine since our college years. Cara and I were both teachers at the school, and she was one of my bridesmaids in our wedding. The five of us coveted to pray that God would lead and direct me to make the right decision concerning the upcoming school year.

Our private Christian school at the time was very small, meaning that the budget for teacher's salaries was the same. By the end of that 2013–2014 school year, we did not have any new students enrolled for the upcoming year other than new kindergarteners whose tuition money would be replacing the tuition for the graduating seniors. This meant that there was no increase in money coming *in* to the school, meaning that there was no way to raise my salary in order for me to make ends meet. (Matthew had clearly been the breadwinner in our home, hands down!) This fact allowed me to make the prayerful decision that God was leading me to resign from teaching. God gave me a measure of comfort in this by bringing my attention to Isaiah 42:16 (KJV). It reads, "And I will bring the blind by a way that they knew not; I will lead them in paths that they have not known: I will make darkness light before them, and crooked things straight. These things will I do unto them, and not forsake them."

As the school year was coming to its close, the same group of five gathered in my pastor's office when I announced my decision. Pastor asked if I would agree to come back if we were able to get some new students over the summer months. I told him that I would *love* to come back. He asked me not to move my things out of the classroom until the end of summer, for that reason, and I gladly agreed. Pastor Ward told me that the school would give me a severance pay. He also announced that he was going to ask our church to give a special "love offering" once a month over the three months of summer, hoping to help me until I could get settled into other employment. These generous special offerings were humbling but so incredibly helpful and appreciated!

I'm not sure that there was a dry eye in that office at the end of our meeting. We sat for several moments and cried. Teaching had been my life! It was what I knew I had been meant to do. It was what I was really *good* at—other than being a wife. (I say this only because Matthew often told me that I was a great wife.) Teaching had given me a feeling of purpose and fulfillment, all the years I had been single. Being a wife gave me purpose and fulfillment while I had a husband. Now I was no longer a schoolteacher and I was no longer a wife. Giving up my twenty-three-year career in teaching felt like another type of death to me.

I was strongly encouraged by my family to go spend some time with my sister Colleen in Tennessee after the school year had ended. When I explained that I had to find a new job, my sister Amy said, "Becky, you can't focus enough to learn *anything* new right now. *You* know that!" She was entirely right. All of my family thought it would be best for me to get away from familiar surroundings for a while so that I could begin to heal. I wasn't even sure, all of a sudden, if I really wanted to remain in our home full of pictures and memories. Colleen and Larry had said that I could stay with their family for as long as I wanted to.

In June, I left for Tennessee, flying out with Colleen, who had come up to see our dad in the nursing home. That spring, Dad had spent his days between the hospital and the nursing home due to his reoccurring blood infection. The last time Dad was hospitalized, he had been in congestive heart failure. Now, he was stable enough to go back to the nursing home yet not strong enough to go back to *his* home.

I stayed with Colleen, Larry, and my nephew and niece, Chase and Leanna, in Tennessee for eighteen days. It was good for me to be away from home and in an unfamiliar place yet with people I loved. Those eighteen days also helped me to know that I *did* want to be back in my home. I actually longed to once again be surrounded by Matthew's memories. During my time in Tennessee, I emailed my first job résumé. I also composed a certain letter that I had read about in one of my books on grief.

One of the authors of a book I had been given made a suggestion for widows and widowers who had experienced a sudden, unexpected loss in which there had been no time to say goodbye. The author recommended that a grieving spouse write a letter to their departed loved one, stating all the things they wished they could have said if they had had a chance to say goodbye. When I came home to Pennsylvania, I sat on the grass at Matthew's graveside and read the letter aloud to him. Of course, I have no way of knowing if he could possibly have heard me or not; but just in case he could, I wanted these things to be said.

July, 2014
My dearest Matthew,

I have wanted to begin this letter to you countless times since the Lord took you to your home in heaven on January 29 of this year. But I've held myself back from doing so because I know that writing this letter is going to be very difficult. There are things I need to say—things I wish so badly that I could tell you. For that reason, I will write them and read them aloud to you. And even though you may never be able to *hear* these words, it may help me to heal a bit by putting my thoughts down on paper.

Matthew, you were the best *gift* God ever gave me in this life other than the gift of my own salvation (and my life had already been richly blessed with family and friends). God brought you into my life—as such an obvious answer to many years of prayer. I know I told you this many times before; but when I would pray for a husband, I would word my prayer in this way, "Lord, if You have a husband for me, please make it so 'crystal clear' that *I* cannot doubt it, *he* cannot doubt it, and *the people who love me* cannot doubt that You sent him to me." I remember telling you that I had seen God do great things for many people, including myself, but that I believe God "outdid Himself" in our situation. There was just no way to question that our Lord designed for you and me to fall in love and marry.

I remember both of us standing in our kitchen, months after we married, talking about how surprisingly well we were adjusting to life together. We had been told that two people in particular wished they could be "flies on the wall" of our home after we became husband and wife. They thought we were going to have some real "down-and-out" fights because we had both been single and had lived alone for so long. We were both very strongly opinionated individuals, and we were used to being able to do things the way we thought they should be done. I remember saying to you, "Matthew, we are doing *really well* adjusting to life together…better than I ever expected!" You smiled and said, "I know! What did Amy and Aaron know when they said they wanted to be flies on the wall?" You had started to turn away, then stopped abruptly, turned to me, and said, "You know, Becky, think about it…the God who created this universe hooked you and me up! It was *bound* to be good!" You also told me repeatedly through our two-year-and-five-month marriage that whenever anyone asked you how married life was, you would proudly reply, "Married life is *great!*"

In almost every one of the 150 some thank-you notes that I wrote following your funeral, I would write, "Matthew was an incredible man and an exceptional husband." I used to deliberately compliment you repeatedly for being such a wonderful husband and for taking such good care of me and making me so happy. I did this for a couple reasons. First of all, your memory at times was so poor that you often forgot things, and I never wanted you to forget how thankful I was for you. But the second reason I did this was because I had told God that if He ever gave me the type of husband I had prayed for, I would make sure to never take that man for granted. And, Matthew, I believe with all my heart that I never did.

You gave me the happiest three years and three months of my entire life! (And I'm counting from the day when we were introduced at the home of Mr. and Mrs. Fry, on our blind date.) God gave me a husband who was more perfectly suited for me than I ever dreamed anyone could be. We both were looking for a spouse who loved the Lord, first and foremost; and we both had some very strong beliefs about God, His Word, and about living our lives to please Him. During the ten months that we dated, we talked on the phone literally for several hundred hours, about almost every subject under the sun. Every time we approached and discussed a spiritual topic which we both knew could be a potential "deal-breaker," we were amazed to find that we were both exactly on the same page. God did that for us, Matthew. We both knew it.

I remember finding out on that Monday evening of October 11, 2010, when we first met, that I was nine years older than you. I didn't expect to hear from you again, yet I knew that you were someone I would surely like to get to know! Later, you told me that you chose not to accept my phone number from Mr. Fry, when he offered it, because you wanted to pray about the age difference first. You said you had perfect peace to pursue things, two days following that blind date. You asked Mr. Fry for my number that Wednesday night at your church service and called me the next evening after work. I was ecstatic!

I was always amazed at how very much we thought alike about so many issues in life, even little things that really didn't matter, just general preferences, and so forth. We were both so particular about so many things; yet even in these preferences, I don't recall there being conflict. (We were quite conscious, however, of the need to compromise from time to time.) And we loved to laugh! Life with you was so *fun*! We laughed with each other nearly every day of our married life. That was definitely one of the highlights of our marriage for me. You commented on it often also. I remember you saying with amazement in your voice, "I sure never expected to make a woman laugh!" There was a time you sent me a text message that read, "You make me laugh. No other woman has ever done that!" We were *perfect* for each other.

I remember telling you that I knew you could have married several different women and would have made any one of them incredibly happy. Yet I told you that I could *guarantee you* that not one of them could have ever loved you as much as I did. I also had told you that I am the kind of person who *loves* deeply, and because of that, I also *hurt* deeply. I suppose that's why I'm not dealing with your loss very well. Matthew, you were the light of my life! From the moment you left for work in the morning, I looked forward to the time we would both be home again at the end of the day. I loved how you found a way to turn your e-mails into text messages while you were at work so that we could communicate throughout the day even though you had no cell phone reception in the underground mine. I loved hearing from you, from my classroom. I miss everything about you, but your voice and our conversations are two of the things I miss the most. Nothing and no one else can fill that void for me.

Matthew, I want you to know that it feels as though my heart now has a large hole ripped inside it, with sharp edges rotating all around. I've been told that the "hole" will always remain, just as my love for you will. But through the course of time, it has been explained that the sharp edges will dull so that the pain will not always be so intense. I've also read that this feeling of loss can be likened to having had my leg amputated. I will *never* walk the same as I once did because such a large part of my life has been removed. Yet I *will* need to learn to walk again. My only hope is to walk with as little a limp as possible.

I want to thank you, Matthew, for being my "dream come true." I will be grateful, every day that I live, that God brought our lives together.

People have told me that they have not seen another married couple show as much open affection toward each other as they saw in you and me. I am so grateful that it was obvious to those around us that we were very much in love. I remember my dad asking you Sunday after Sunday, during our first months of marriage, "Well, Matthew, is the honeymoon over yet?" You'd smile, grab me in a big hug, and say, "*No! The honeymoon isn't over!*" I finally asked my dad to stop asking you that question because I *never* wanted our honeymoon to be over…and nearly two-and-a-half years later, it wasn't.

Although every day for the past five months, I have wished that God chose to take both of us to heaven together; the fact of the matter is that He didn't. And although I wish I knew why our time on earth together had to be entirely too short, I cannot possibly know. I realize I have to trust that God has something more here for me to do. But the wonderful promise that I cling to from the Bible is that one beautiful day, I will get to join you in the only place I truly desire to be. I love that I have no doubt whatsoever that you are in heaven. I know that because you shared your testimony with me during one of the first conversations we ever had. You told me about the day that you asked Christ to forgive your sins and to be your personal Lord and Savior. You told me that that day changed your life. Then two months after we married, you even took me to Edinboro University and gave me a tour of the campus. That tour ended with a walk to an upper level of the campus library, where you pointed out the place you believed you were sitting on the night you were saved. How thankful I am that I will never have to wonder where you are spending eternity. I only have to wonder when I get to join you.

I love that God had so graciously given us a long snowy weekend that stretched into the early morning hours of that Wednesday that you entered heaven. I love that He gave us so much quality time alone during those last four days. I love that we went to bed that last night, completely content in our love for each other. And I love that you teased me in our final conversation, saying, "You'd better watch it or I'll bounce you right out of bed!" God allowed you to finish your life on this earth with no pain. He let you fall asleep next to the wife who you promised to love for the rest of your life and then awaken about one hour and twenty minutes later, to your Lord up in heaven.

I love you, Matthew William Yount! And I thank you for letting *me* know what it feels like to be fully and completely loved. I have cried so many tears over missing you that I fear the blue eyes that you loved may eventually have their color washed away. But, Matthew, I know you would want me to walk on. I know you would want me to finish my course, as you so beautifully finished yours. I cannot tell you that I'm not struggling, Matthew, but I can tell you that with God's help, I plan to finish my life *well*. You have shown me how to do just that, and you are and will remain my inspiration.

I love you, Matthew. I will forever and always be thankful that God allowed me to share my life with you. I am so blessed that God let me be the one who got to love you!

With all my love, until we meet again,
Your Becky

# Chapter 32

I came home from Tennessee on the fifth of July. On the twenty-second of that same month, my dad was taken to Butler Memorial Hospital again. He had become consistently tired and increasingly weak. We were told that the blood infection had settled into the artificial valve site inside Dad's heart. It was obvious that he was far too weak to undergo open-heart surgery again. He had gone through that surgery twice before, once at the age of sixty and again at seventy. Instead, Dad was scheduled for a blood transfusion to see if that would help.

Two days later would be the date that Matthew would have celebrated his thirty-eighth birthday, if he had still been here with us. I had asked Matthew's closest family members if they would be willing to get together with me so that we could remember him together. Matthew's aunt Sue and uncle Tony opened their home to us. Matthew's brother, Michael; our sister-in-law, Amy; our nephew, Aidan; and nieces, Kathleen, Lindsay, and Claire traveled from Florida to be here. They joined my mother-in-law, father-in-law, Matthew's grandma, his uncle Bill, and me. We did nothing other than look at some pictures and talk and eat, really. I just knew that we would all be hurting on that difficult day, and I had hoped it would be a bit easier if we hurt together instead of separately. I believe that it helped a little.

Because it was an emotional day, I had asked beforehand if I could spend the night at Matthew's folks' home in Conway and travel back to Butler the next day. That next morning, Matthew's family and I went out to breakfast together. It was while we were in the restaurant, during a phone call home, that I was told my father had taken a turn for the worst. I came back to the table, unable to hide my emotions. I bid goodbye to my in-laws, the people who had played such important roles in my dear husband's life. Then I left for home.

My sister Colleen was also called. She was told that she should come home, if she had hopes of seeing Dad again. She boarded a plane in Tennessee.

Four days later, my dad was ushered by the angels into heaven. Pneumonia had settled into his lungs around the time of that blood transfusion. He was too weak to fight any longer.

I would be remiss if I did not share with you one beautiful memory of my dad's final day on earth. During his last couple months, Dad's compelling wish was to go to church one more time. But no matter how hard he had worked, he no longer had strength enough to walk out of the nursing home and to the car…or from the car into the church building. My dad was such a strong faithful Christian. For the last several decades of his life, Dad didn't miss church services unless he was entirely too sick to attend. Now for over four-and-a-half months, he had not been able to gather on the Lord's Day with his church family, whom he dearly loved.

Our former pastor, Wayne Dillabaugh, now buys and sells vehicles for a living. While Dad was still at the nursing home, this former preacher of ours told us that he would purchase a wheelchair-accessible vehicle, if we were able to gain permission to take Dad to church. He explained that he could sell the vehicle later. The nursing home granted permission, and arrangements for the vehicle were lined up. My family was overwhelmed with gratitude and my dad was filled with excitement and determination. When the goal-date of Sunday, July 20, had arrived, however, it had become impossible for my father to make the trip to church. The next day, he was hospitalized for the final time.

Dad's last full day on earth was the very next Sunday, July 27. He would spend it in the intensive care unit of the hospital. My dad's beautiful bright-blue eyes remained incredibly alert as member after member of our beloved "church family" began to file in to Dad's hospital room, young and old, family after family. Some of the most precious friends Dad had ever been blessed with in his lifetime surrounded his hospital bed. The room was filled with love and compassion as we sang together many of my dad's favorite hymns. Dad was no longer able to speak, let alone sing, but that didn't matter so much. His eyes showed heartfelt appreciation as we sang the chorus that most all of us knew was his favorite, called "Let the Lord have His Way." No, my dad did not make it to church one more time, but many from our church made it to *him*. My dad knew he was loved. I happen to believe that this is because *my dad* knew how to love.

Eleven minutes after midnight, my heavenly Father chose to take my earthly father to his home in heaven. The date was July 28, 2014. My dear daddy passed through the pearly gates of heaven at the age of seventy-nine, following his son-in-law Matthew by one day shy of six months.

# Chapter 33

My heart hurt so badly that I did not feel it could take any more. Yet in spite of only wanting to be in heaven with the two men I had loved most in this life, I had to "get it together" enough to find new employment. It was nearing the end of summer. The last of the special offerings that had so graciously been collected for me by my church family would be given in August. And for the first time since I had completed my final year of college, I was no longer employed as an elementary schoolteacher.

Once again, the Lord provided.

On the first Tuesday of September 2014, I started my new part-time job working as a receptionist at a law office only minutes from my house. My friend Karen had helped me to get this temporary job. The attorney only wanted someone to help out for a few hours a day, a few days a week, mainly to answer phones. I needed something to keep me occupied and to begin bringing in some kind of income. Wouldn't you know, God arranged for my first day of work to also be the first day of school at my beloved Calvary Academy. The timing could not have been more perfect.

On the *last* Tuesday of that *same* month of September 2014, I began my second new job. This one was full-time, with health benefits! I would be selling jewelry in the fine jewelry department of Boscov's Department Store. I would work both the part-time job at the attorney's office and the full-time job at Boscov's, for nearly nine months. Then I decided that it might be all right to allow myself a little free time instead of working so much.

Matthew would have smiled to see that I was regularly permitted to handle and try on gold, gemstones, and diamonds. He knew how much I enjoy pretty jewelry! This second job, which I worked for just under six years, gave me the opportunity to work with some special ladies who I never would have gotten to know otherwise. These ladies, who I once considered only to be my "coworkers," have become friends who I truly care about. I also became acquainted with a large handful of favorite customers whose kind words and smiles helped to make my days brighter.

The most surprising and interesting benefit of being employed at Boscov's, however, is the fact that, through it, I had the opportunity to meet and get to know a best-selling author who worked there for a time. When I overheard that we had an author working in our midst, I introduced myself and, soon after, took a class that he taught on how to write a book. Although I had wanted to write a book of my own for as long as I can remember, I had never known anyone who had written one. I also didn't have the slightest idea of how to get started. Now, my excuses were gone!

It turns out that Mr. Timothy Ayers has authored many books, including a series of children's mystery books that have been read by many of my own former students of Calvary Academy! They were extremely popular choices when my third- and fourth-graders were learning how to write their first book reports!

I do not believe in coincidences. I feel certain that God knew all along that I needed to meet someone who could help me get this book started. I believe that God intentionally placed me where I needed to be in order to meet a published best-selling author...in a very unlikely place.

# Chapter 34

For over three solid years after losing Matthew, only a small handful of days would pass in which I did not cry. I know this because I remember becoming fearful that I would never begin to heal from my great losses. Upon reaching the three-year mark of Matthew's passing, I actually documented the fact that I still cried every day. On more than one occasion, I went to my bedroom closet, where Matthew's newest Carhartt coat still hung on a hanger. I wanted to feel his arms around me so badly that I leaned into his coat, wrapped the empty sleeves around me, and sobbed.

I now know what it is like to lose my husband *and* my father. And although I loved both of them tremendously and miss both of them greatly, the losses are very different. I realize that Matthew and I were not married all that long. But we had waited so long to *find* each other, and we were constantly amazed at how perfectly suited we were for each other. We were so happy together (maybe not every *moment*, but certainly every *day*)! Those who spent much time at all with us could see how very much we were in love. Comments were often made to that fact.

I miss *talking* to Matthew. I deeply miss our conversations. It wasn't until marriage that I realized just how differently men and women communicate. There are some exceptions, to be sure; but as a whole, we women are so emotional. Men seem to be so *logical*. Many times, I would be upset or confused about one thing or another and would talk to Matthew about it. Without fail, he would lay out some facts that made perfect sense, and I would see the situation much more clearly. I just hadn't been able to see it that way on my own. I *always* felt better after talking things over with him. I *miss* having my husband's perspective on life's situations.

Actually, I miss every single aspect of marriage. I miss Matthew's hugs, which made me feel like nothing in the world could ever harm me. I sincerely miss his kisses and the feeling of his hand holding mine. I miss falling asleep, snuggled up beside him in bed, and I miss seeing his sleepy smile when I awake in the morning. I miss those looks that couples share, revealing that one knew just what the other was thinking. I miss dreaming together about what we hoped to do in the years to come. But the one thing I miss, most of all, is the feeling of being *loved* completely by someone—of *belonging* completely to someone. Matthew was mine and I was his. When I lost him, I not only lost my husband. I lost my partner, my lover, my confidante, my best friend.

I said all that to say that *the number of years* a couple has been married is not what makes the difference in how sorely one grieves their spouse's loss. The *love and connection* shared between that couple determine the depth of our sadness when our spouse has been removed from our lives. That feeling of loss is only *compounded* when no chance was given to say goodbye.

I recall going to have my taxes done for the first time after Matthew had passed away. Our CPA is a lady who had done Matthew's taxes for many years before we married. When she was extending her condolences to me, Wendy said, "I remember the first time you both came in here together." She added, "Matthew looked *happy*. He finally looked *whole*." She chose the word "whole"! I thought that was beautiful. "Whole" is what I never feel any longer.

Matthew was an awesome fun-loving uncle. I feel certain that all eight of our nephews and nieces would agree with that description. He loved to play with the kids and he *loved* to tease. Yet although we had desperately wanted children of our own, Matthew and I had been unable to become parents. Most times now, I still wish that I had a child of ours here with me. Yet knowing how hard it has been for me to deal with the loss of my husband, I think God knew that it would have perhaps been too difficult for me to raise our child by myself. I believe I would always have felt inadequate knowing what a good father Matthew would have been.

Because I had been left without my husband and without having had children, other plans for my future appeared to have come to an end as well. Matthew and I had planned several vacations that we wanted to take in the many years ahead. Without him, I no longer had someone to travel with.

Two girlfriends changed that for me, however! These ladies were already two of my closest friends, all of us right around the same age and members of the same church. Karen and I had been teachers in side-by-side classrooms at school. She had been the photographer in our wedding. Cindy plays the piano beautifully and was the pianist in our wedding. Both of them had children that were already raised and out of the house, and these ladies no longer had anyone to go on big vacations with either.

Two-and-a-half years after Matthew passed away, Cindy, Karen, and I had saved up enough money to go on a cruise to Bermuda—one of the trips on Matthew's and my wish list. Of course, I shed some tears in private each day, but we had a really wonderful time. Since then, the three of us took a short trip to the Canadian side of Niagara Falls; and we have definite plans of going on other vacations together in the years to come. What a blessing!

# Chapter 35

I have now passed the seven-year anniversary of the day that Matthew entered eternity. And usually, it still feels like I lost him such a *short* time ago. Even though I no longer cry every day and even though some definite progress has been made toward my healing, I am absolutely and positively certain that I am forever altered. I am not exactly the same person I was when I had Matthew here with me. I see things differently. I feel things more deeply. Even happy times have a subtle note of sadness behind them…simply because he is not present to share those moments with me. But I once again can see the sunshine! And that hasn't always been the case.

Strangely enough, I actually believe that I am a richer person for having gone through deep heartache and great grief. I find that I now possess a large amount of compassion for others who are hurting. I also take notice of those who are lonely in a way I never did before. Honestly, I never *realized* how very many hurting people there are in our world. I never *noticed* how many *lonely* people there are around us either. My life is still very blessed to have a wonderful loving support system, comprised of many people who would drop what they were doing and be there for me if they knew that I needed them. I now realize that there are many people who have *no one*…or at least they *feel like* they have no one.

Of course, I had known other women who had lost their husbands years ago. I remember feeling sorry for them in their losses. If truth be told, however, I didn't hurt for them for long. I figured that they would soon *get over it*. Now, I am ashamed to realize how very wrong I had been. I have come to *despise* the phrase "get over it" when used in reference to the loss of someone dearly loved. None of us "get over it." We learn to "adjust" and to carry on in *spite* of our losses.

As achingly hard as this road through grief continues to be, I cannot help but see moments of God's graciousness when I look back. I see it in Matthew's and my truly happy marriage. I see it especially in the last four days of our time on earth together. With all the frigid cold and the snow that had covered our area from Matthew's last Saturday through that final Tuesday night, most of our ordinary plans had been canceled. I believe with all my heart that this was God's deliberate way of rearranging our normally busy and heavily scheduled lives. Instead, He made a way to give this husband and wife four days filled with unexpected hours to spend alone together, almost snowbound, in our home. You know, it felt a bit like another honeymoon. I even see moments of God's graciousness when I think of the fact that God allowed Matthew to awaken, only a little more than an hour before he would take his last breath. And it warms my heart when I remember that Matthew's final words made me laugh.

If I had to do it all again, I would not trade one second of having had Matthew in my life. Some people search their entire lives for the kind of love that Matthew and I shared. I genuinely believe that we had more love in our short marriage than a whole lot of people ever experience in a lifetime. *I have been richly blessed!*

No, I may not agree with God's decision to take my husband from me when we felt that the happiest chapter in our lives had only begun. But God is still God. He has every right to do as He pleases with His creation. We do not always get to *see* His reasoning, and it is not our job to *agree* with His choices. It is our job to *trust* that "as for God, his way is perfect," as the Bible states in Psalm 18:30 (KJV).

Additionally, I cannot ignore one particular glaring fact. I would never have been blessed to have had Matthew in my life at all, if it had not been for that same God who chose to take Matthew to heaven so suddenly. And I am eternally grateful that I *know* that my Matthew's sins had been forgiven so that he can indeed *be in* heaven today. Because I, too, have been born again, I have the promise from

God's Word that I will get to see Matthew again when I join him there.

God did not *have to* let me meet, or marry, Matthew William Yount. Yet I will be *forever* deeply happy that He did.

You see, OURS was a love worth waiting for!

And together they built a life they loved.

—Anonymous

CPSIA information can be obtained
at www.ICGtesting.com
Printed in the USA
BVHW062330091122
651488BV00003B/6

9 781638 743859